Productivity Measurement
and Incentives

PRODUCTION ENGINEERING SERIES

General Editor
Norman A Dudley PhD
Lucas Professor of Engineering Production
The University of Birmingham

The Institution of Production Engineers defines a production engineer as 'one who is competent by reason of education, training and experience to determine the factors involved in the manufacture of commodities, and to direct the production processes to achieve the most efficient coordination of effort, with due regard to quantity, quality and cost'. The quest for such competence is a formidable task in view of the range of contributing disciplines and the rate of development of production engineering and production management techniques. This series of books is intended to contribute to the more efficient utilisation of technical, economic and human resources in industry by presenting a reappraisal of the objectives and techniques of current practice and an assessment of the practical implications of relevant research findings.

Productivity Measurement and Incentives

R. G. NORMAN,
MSc CEng FIProdE MIMechE AMBIM

S. BAHIRI,
MSc Phd CEng MIProdE MIWSP AMBIM

LONDON
BUTTERWORTHS

THE BUTTERWORTH GROUP

ENGLAND
Butterworth & Co (Publishers) Ltd
London: 88 Kingsway, WC2B 6AB

AUSTRALIA
Butterworth & Co (Australia) Ltd
Sydney: 586 Pacific Highway Chatswood, NSW 2067
Melbourne: 343 Little Collins Street, 3000
Brisbane: 240 Queen Street, 4000

CANADA
Butterworth & Co (Canada) Ltd
Toronto: 14 Curity Avenue, 374

NEW ZEALAND
Butterworth & Co (New Zealand) Ltd
Wellington: 26–28 Waring Taylor Street, 1

SOUTH AFRICA
Butterworth & Co (South Africa) (Pty) Ltd
Durban: 152–154 Gale Street

First published in 1972
© Butterworth & Co (Publishers) Ltd, 1972

ISBN 0 408 70308 3 Standard
     0 408 70309 1 Limp

Printed in England by Willmer Brothers Ltd., Birkenhead

Foreword

Unless a manufacturing concern employs productivity measures which are meaningful for itself and for others in the same industry, it is in no position to assess its present or its potential level of efficiency. Unfortunately there is little agreement among industrial executives as to what are the criteria in designing productivity indices, and the theorists are equally divided.

Measures are needed to quickly highlight inefficiencies within organisations and their constituent departments so that remedial action can be taken.

Part 1 of this volume presents a critical examination of various measures of productivity which have been advocated and their theoretical and practical implications.

Part 2 reports on the first stage of an investigation in which the authors played a prominent part, undertaken in West Midlands industry to measure productive efficiency and which led to a questioning of the Census of Production statistics and their interpretation.

Part 3 presents and discusses the contribution and the limitations of work measurement and incentives in agreements aimed at promoting industrial productivity.

Norman A. Dudley
Lucas Professor of Engineering Production
University of Birmingham

Preface

Manufacturing is a process of converting raw material into useful products, but in this process there are complex interactions among the factors involved. These complexities cannot be simplified until more adequate costing systems are integrated with productivity measurement. While normally being aware of the physical measures of plant level resource utilisation, the production engineer frequently lacks understanding of the measures used by economists (net output per employee) and accountants (return on capital employed). These measures tend now to be used more than engineering standards to interpret productivity.

Following a macro analysis of several industries in the West Midlands we found that for short term analysis, net output per employee and indeed other ratios used by accountants and economists can be misleading. For instance, in 1966 the Board of Trade published some of their regional Census of Production statistics which for 1958 indicated that the metalworking and engineering industries, (which occupy 40% of West Midlands employment as against 20% nationally) had a net output per employee of 96% of the corresponding average for Great Britain and that only two regions, the East and West Ridings of Yorkshire and the North West, had lower indices of productivity.

Subsequently, a Productivity Research Unit sponsored by the Department of Economic Affairs was established in the Department of Engineering Production of Birmingham University to investigate the causes of these below average figures. Whilst we found insufficient evidence to show that the West Midlands real productivity was low, it was established that utilisation productivity of labour and machines was often only half what it could be.

In our approach to productivity measurement in this book we have endeavoured to be sufficiently plausible for the business entrepreneur, sophisticated for the academic and appealing to the production engineer, accountant and economist. We say appealing because it is these professions that need to show more co-ordination and innovation by improving management information systems that will provide adequate criteria on which manufacturing decisions can be made.

The book is arranged in three parts, the first being concerned with a critical review of the methods used to assess productivity. Included in an appendix to Part 1 is an introduction to Interfirm Comparisons for Management contributed by Taylor Harrington and Ingham.

Part II is an account of the research carried out in twenty-four metalworking and engineering companies in the West Midlands. A new statistical sampling method 'Disc-O-Tec' is introduced which was found to be more convenient than orthodox methods.

Part III is a review of the economic, social and motivational aspects of incentives.

The contents of the book are intended for students of production engineering and works management, and considered suitable for C.E.I., Degree, Business Diploma and National Diploma course work and examinations. Equally, it will provide economists, accountants and business entrepreneurs with an understanding of the essentials of productivity measurement, costing and incentives, against which to compare their own company performances. For productivity research workers, a comprehensive reference list is included.

R.G.N.
S.B.

Acknowledgements

While it is not possible to mention all those individuals, companies and government departments who have co-operated in these studies we hope that in naming only those to whom we are particularly indebted, our remaining colleagues will understand that we are not unmindful of their contribution. Indeed without their advice and assistance the completion of this work would have been impossible.

We gratefully acknowledge the assistance of the foremen and operatives of more than a score of industrial companies. The foremen, particularly, contributed by willingly carrying out—in addition to their normal duties —systematic observation of the activities of men and machines under their control. Thanks are also due to the Department of Trade and Industry for the attention given to our many difficult enquiries.

We are also indebted to Professor Norman Dudley, Director of the Productivity Research Unit, Dr. Brian Jenney and Ian Puzey, our colleagues at Birmingham University, Professor Harold Martin of the Reneselaer Polytechnic Institute, New York, Geoffrey A. Colley of the former Department of Economic Affairs and Alfred Mendoza of the Department of Trade and Industry.

R.G.N.
S.B.

Contents

Chapter 1

Productivity as a Common Objective

The Government may be looked upon as the guardian of national
economic enterprise, and through its organisational complex it can
influence a variety of regional, industrial and company economic
planning policies with the objective of promoting growth, profits
and earnings potential which ensure a continuing improvement in
the standard of living.

It is one of the responsibilities of the Government to apportion
degrees of importance to priorities—but real ultimate success
depends upon the co-operation of employers and trade unions.
In the last resort, the Government has the responsibility for ensuring
that limited sectional interests do not frustrate the achievement of
an agreed growth objective.[1]

The improvement of productivity in industry is an agreed
common objective, and on the eve of the National Productivity
Conference in 1967, the Right Honourable Harold Wilson,[2] wrote:

'exhortation and appeals alone cannot increase productivity.
It requires firm decisions and action taken by Government,
Management and Unions. The Government's role is to shape the
economy, so that increased productivity is encouraged and is
rewarded. Management's contribution is to take initiatives to
plan ahead and to show enterprise—above all to innovate.
Unions must look ahead, accept change, particularly in long
established practices, and themselves suggest and sponsor
innovation. The rewards for the nation for higher productivity
will be high.'

Mr. Wilson gave a recipe of general aims directed towards
improved national economic growth, and the understanding of

1

this recipe by all parties will create a significant contribution to increased output per head.

1.1 PRODUCTIVITY INTERPRETATIONS

It is generally acknowledged that 'output per head' in British industry is low in comparison with foreign performances. Maddison, cited by Jones and Barnes[3] claims: 'British industrial productivity is now below that of all West European countries north of the Alps', and: 'throughout industry we are misusing labour, employing too many men to the job and allowing much of their time to be deliberately and systematically wasted'. Most observers agree with such statements and it is obvious that the economic situation is such that improvement in productivity is an urgent task. However, before comparisons of productivity can be reliably drawn, existing productivity measures and other 'output per head' indices need to be examined for their adequacy.

Productivity and production are often regarded as synonymous. An improvement in production may be obtained simply by increasing the resources producing it such as:

(1) increasing the labour force
(2) working additional hours
(3) providing more capital and equipment

But by increasing such resources productivity may well be sacrificed. Figures of production tell how much is produced, while productivity tells how well the resources have been used in producing it. Wells[4] writes: 'production is the activity of converting units of input into units of output, but productivity is measured as a relationship between the two'.

Productivity in its broadest sense is generally viewed as a more intensive use of conversion resources, such as labour and machines, and if measured on a factual basis should indicate reliably performance or efficiency. However the interpretation of such measures is inconsistent and presents a confused and perplexing subject.

Productivity literature generously supported by facts and case studies, abounds with definitions contributed by economists, accountants, engineers, politicians and trade unionists—each projecting a view that best suits his own perspective. Whilst some reports contribute significantly to the library of literature, a large proportion is published only to proclaim a fruitful work study investigation—often restricted to a narrow sector of one firm. Most publications unfortunately limit the discussions to comparisons of labour productivity and ignore the productivity of machines. As industry becomes more capital intensive it may be argued that it is machinery rather than (or in conjunction with) labour that generates output per head.

In this era of technological change industry is becoming more capital intensive and it would appear that the proportion of labour costs to those of total manufacturing costs is diminishing. Rostas[5] writes: 'In industries where this (labour) proportion is small and the proportion of other factors in total costs high, the measurement in labour productivity only may not lead us very far without the measurement of productivity of other factors'. Output per head is dependent upon how capital as well as the total input resources of a system is used.

Since little headway has been made in measuring capital productivity, or even labour and capital productivity in a combined form, comparisons between firms within given industries will continue to be inconsistent and misleading.

Chapter 2

Accountants' Measures of Productivity

There is an abundance of crude financial and productivity measures in existence, but many are unable to satisfy the essential yardstick that they are sufficiently plausible for the business entrepreneur and refined enough for the production engineer/manager.

Many of the productivity measures used today are those developed by accountants and are financially orientated. There are firms that attempt to evaluate the worth and effectiveness of business activities by adopting 'financial ratio analysis'—ratios that provide management with valuable pointers in terms of liquidity, funds and profitability.

Theoretically, there are no limits to the number of ratios that can be derived. Foulke[6] suggests that five hundred or more can be made. However the important factor is whether the relationship is useful. Such measures are broadly concerned with the 'sales return on capital employed' or 'profit to assets' ratios, which have often been referred to as a measure of business efficiency and occasionally by some company executives as a measure of productivity. Some examples are listed below:

$$\text{Current (liquidity) ratio} = \frac{\text{Current asset value}}{\text{Current liabilities}} \tag{2.1}$$

where current assets include cash, marketable securities, accounts receivable and useful inventories. Current liabilities include accounts outstanding, bank overdrafts, accrued expenses and tax liabilities.

$$\text{Inventory turnover} = \frac{\text{Sales value}}{\text{Average inventory}} \tag{2.2}$$

a ratio that indicates the number of times the average inventory is turned over in a given period.

$$\text{Return on assets} \quad = \frac{\text{Net profit} + \text{Interest}}{\text{Total assets}} \qquad (2.3)$$

a ratio that appraises profitability, but is highly suspect because asset value may well be under valued, and often includes such intangibles as goodwill and patents.

$$\text{Return on sales} \quad = \frac{\text{Net profit}}{\text{Sales}} \qquad (2.4)$$

a ratio that appraises the efficiency of operations, where pricing and the volume of sales may affect its reliability.

The objective of most financial measures is to provide management with a set of signposts. In the revitalisation of G.E.C's operations Weinstock set out seven key ratios to control the operational aspects of a decentralised complex.[7]

(1) Profit/Capital employed
(2) Profit/Sales
(3) Sales/Capital employed
(4) Sales/Fixed assets
(5) Sales/Stocks
(6) Sales/Employee
(7) Profits/Employee

The use of such ratios is not new and goes back to the nineteen twenties.[8] They can be useful but it should be understood that what is being compared can be misleading unless interpreted with care.

Witschey[9] writes: 'Accounting neither strives for nor attains absolute truth. Although it is characterised by a rather elaborate theoretical framework, its results are usually dependent upon judgement. While there are limited objectives in accounting, perhaps its principal purpose is to describe change. Thus in the case of a business entity the central goal of accounting is the determination of income (or expenditure), i.e. changes resulting from the efficiency of operations'.

Closer examination of the ratios show that they are sales orientated, and yet the sales value (and hence the profit) may have nothing to do with the efficiency of production but may be strongly influenced by supply and demand. Even when selling prices are normally based on operating costs (and these are often found to be anomalous), it is a common practice for profit to be added as a percentage of the total costs, costs which include material and other external purchases that already contain the suppliers profit margin. So it becomes obvious that the value of the material used has a strong influence on the sales and profit margins, and thus on the productivity ratios of a company.

In most calculations the value of assets taken is usually that value occurring at the end of a financial period—and most generally that of a Book value—while the profit and sales values are derived from the amount of income received over the whole period. Consequently, unless the value of the asset has remained stable during the reference period, or is the average of the asset value over the reference period, the rate must be suspect because of the different time basis used. Furthermore, Book values may have no relationship to the actual asset values or their replacement costs today. This will affect depreciation costs which are charged against profits and consequently the return on capital employed.

The authors research found that depreciation policies varied greatly. Book value depreciation was on average 52% that of the realistic written down replacement value depreciation and varied from 10% to 100% of the realistic assessment. Insurance (or capital protection costs) values of assets were on average 2.5 times the Book values and 1.25 times the written down replacement values. Written down replacement values varied from 25% to 333% of the insured values while Book values varied between 11% and 100% of insured values. Consequently each company follows its own valuation policy and often makes decisions on inaccurate information.

The Plessey Co. recognised the disadvantages of certain depreciation practices when in the first quarter of the financial year 1969, they revised their accounting practices by charging depreciation to profits in the quarter in which the asset was introduced, rather than for the whole year. This tended to eliminate the former disproportionate heavy charge of depreciation in a single annual period. In the same company another important change occurred concerning the Government investment grants. These are now deducted from the cost of the asset before depreciation which consequently reduces the depreciation charge. Other forward looking companies have carried out this practice for some time.

To overcome some of the inadequacies, the use of replacement value accounting practised by several firms provides an improved index—an index unfortunately still unable to satisfy the total objectives of the organisation. It can for instance have the ludicrous result of demonstrating that the most profitable part of the business (using an old and cheap machine) should be shut down. Where replacement cost is impossible to calculate, for example the value of assets that may have been improved or remodelled, as found in the fastener industry—bolts, nuts, screws and rivets—an assumed current cost might be a practical compromise.

Sizer[10] argues: 'depreciation should be calculated on the assumed current cost of fixed assets and not on the basis of historical cost', he suggests that this could be derived three ways:

(1) By the use of accepted indices, such as those calculated by the Economist Intelligence Unit. These are available as a single index for industrial plant or in a number of separate indices for main groups of assets
(2) By formal revaluation undertaken by professional valuers or by competent officials of the company at regular intervals of time
(3) By the substitution of current values as declared for fire insurance purposes.

From what has already been discussed revaluation is the more reliable.

Financial ratio analysis now plays a prominent part in management policy and decision making. Ingham and Taylor Harrington[11] have arranged a collection of simple but comprehensive measures into a logically constructed framework, the presentation resembling a pyramid of ratios. They were originally devised to help general management understand the way in which certain business factors determine their firm's return on assets employed. The framework has since been effectively used to present a channel of information between the technical levels of a company and its general management. All the ratios are interdependent so that management can test the implications of change and prevent the need for arbitrary and misleading decisions. An account of Interfirm Comparisons for Management contributed by Ingham and Taylor Harrington is included as an appendix to Part I of this volume.

2.1 COST ACCOUNTING CONCEPTS

The amount of attention paid by production managers, systems analysts and engineers to developing improved bases for decision making and control leaves much to be desired, despite the fact that their work involves and depends upon data developed from costing

B

and budgetary systems. Even though engineers/managers may occasionally complain about the adequacy of the data, in fact the very nature of the information they receive is a function of the adequacy of the costing system from which their information is derived.

Developing a costing system is too important a function to be left entirely to the traditional cost accountant, but should involve partnership with the engineering management functions. The main objectives of cost accounting are:

(1) Accurately to ascertain costs of products and processes under differing conditions and systems concepts
(2) Provide bases for effective control of costs in every form of economic and engineering activity
(3) Provide reliable information for sound management decision making

While historical costing systems collect data on expenditures and apply them to products at the end of some fiscal period, standard costing systems attempt to predetermine product costs and to use these as standards for cost control purposes.

However useful Standard Costing and Budgetary Control techniques might be, (and even such techniques are often inadequately employed), since they are based on comparing actual results to some budgeted performance, they do not reveal the potential utilisations of labour and machines.

Probably the most prevalent costing system used in industry is the labour based overhead absorption system where the total costs of operating an enterprise (excluding direct materials which are costed separately) are allocated to the amount of direct labour, hours or costs, which it is anticipated will be used in production during the fiscal period. Usually this type of system does not distinguish between capital intensive and labour intensive cost centres. The costing rate per labour hour is derived by dividing the total operating expenses by the total direct labour hours, or by some other means such as floor space.

An improved system could be to apportion the overhead expenses to separate work stations, based on an attempt to determine their relative share of the total operating expenses for the fiscal period, and to divide these apportionments by the pertinent anticipated or predicted work station utilisations. Thus for two work stations of equal weight, the first operating for twice the hours of the second, the first would have a process cost rate of one half the other. The individual work station or cost centre hourly rate would be:

$$\frac{\text{total anticipated cost of operating centre per period}}{\text{total anticipated hours usage of centre per period}} \quad (2.5)$$

One of the weaknesses of such a system would be that since product costs would vary with the overall fluctuation in the use of facilities, that is, with overall sales, the profitability of particular products made at different levels of system utilisation would seem to vary as between fiscal periods. Such variations (being features not of the products but of the levels of system activity at the time of their manufacture) would tend adversely to influence the effectiveness of management decisions concerned with the relative merits of alternative products as means for satisfying system objectives.

Direct or marginal costing avoids the complications entailed in predicting future levels of activity and of making apportionments, based thereon, of the unavoidable period costs to the products made during future accounting periods. This is done through the device of percentage overhead charges on product direct labour or machine hours and costs. Only direct costs, judged to be unavoidable by not producing specific products are charged to the products. The margin of sales income S, in excess of the direct avoidable costs V, for each product, or product group, is assumed to be a reliable indication of the relative advantage of producing one product as compared to another in seeking to achieve optimal operation of the system. The cost of operating fixed production facilities are not chargeable to any particular product, and are not related to the level of utilisation of the various facilities incurred in making such products. Inferentially, in direct or marginal costing, it is assumed (probably erroneously) that the rate at which contribution margin (the sales value minus variable expenses or $S - V = CM$) is generated per unit of time or cost of occupancy of the production facilities is the same for all products.

Under utilised capacity machines, as well as incurring more capital expenditure, generally occupying more space and having higher operating costs, are charged as if they were operating under optimum conditions, and being the correct machine for the job. Obviously, this method of charging is necessary to recover production costs, but in order to identify any deficiency it would appear that a utilisation index—Potential/Actual—should be built into management costing systems, which would then indicate an optimised condition of operation. Instances are known of a 'running' utilisation index in some of the more progressive companies costing systems, but as yet no company has shown innovation by including an 'occupancy' utilisation index. Only one company, an electrical engineering manufacturer accounts for an 'intensity' factor incorporated in a 'technical' index which represents the ideal minimum throughput time. More is said about this improvement in Chapter 3.

'Accountants and Educators alike, have been and still are seeking the answer to many perplexing questions. They are concerned about the difficulties involved in comparing financial statements, even those of companies in the same industry, because of the diversity and inconsistency in the application of accounting principles and practices'.[9]

Even if the Labour Government's proposal[12] that certain sorts of information should be made available to employee representatives, this would not necessarily lead to a better understanding as to how companies are run, or encourage greater participation unless the accounting information is coupled with some move towards educating the employees and their representatives as to the significance of the information. At present it is difficult to be optimistic that this would be adequately implemented for employee representatives when one sees how little managers and accountants really understand about the meaning of such data.

It is obvious that there is room for more constructive measures, or ratios, possibly along the lines of 'Productivity Costing and Control' formulated by Martin[13] which would permit plant level productivity to be measured in financial terms whilst at the same time taking account of all factor inputs and their utilisations.

2.2 PRODUCTIVITY COSTING

Productivity Costing was developed to improve methods of cost accounting, cost control and particularly managerial decision making. The intention was to avoid many of the pitfalls of both conventional overhead absorption and marginal costing. Productivity Costing may be considered as an operating expense absorption costing method in which products absorb materials conversion costs at a rate based on the facilities capacity to produce rather than an ability to sell products[14]. Alternatively it may be considered as a marginal costing system in which due proportions of the fixed costs are absorbed by products according to their use of productive facilities, at a costing rate based on the maximum feasible use of the facilities.

As a system, productivity costing is compatible with standard, absorption and marginal costing methods, and special systems integrating these concepts may be designed specifically to meet the organisational and functional requirements of any particular enterprise.

The major objective of industrial-commercial systems is assumed to be the maximisation of total earnings T or of the rate of generating total earnings per unit of total conversion costs C, thereby maximising T/C. Consequently while the primary productivity index is derived from T/C, the rate of profit generation is the ratio of profit P to conversion costs C or P/C. Since profit is the difference between total earnings and conversion costs $T-C = P$, the secondary productivity index will be:

$$\frac{P}{C} = \frac{T-C}{C} = \frac{T}{C} - 1 \tag{2.6}$$

In maximising the primary productivity index T/C the secondary index P/C is also maximised since it is always unity less than the total earnings productivity.

The most common measure of productivity has been the physical unit of product output (sales or added value) per input factor (mainly labour). Productivity Costing, while representing the system's engineering view of productivity measurement, aims at reducing all inputs and outputs into economic values, or monetary terms.

An output is generated (or value added) only by the utilised inputs, and it may be conceptualised that the ratio of utilised inputs to total inputs available (which cannot exceed unity) is a measure of the efficiency, or productivity of the system. The total conversion cost inputs required to add value to throughput materials in order to convert into saleable products, is the product cost C_d. Since the cost of operating the entire system C_s includes the non utilised, or idle costs C_i (which are not allocated to the products in productivity costing) the conversion utilisation, or productivity would be C_d/C_s.

The potential total earnings, T_{pot}, generated by a given system's input C_s, is equal to the total earnings T, that could have been generated if all the inputs had been fully utilised. This is equal to the sum product total earnings productivity for all products produced $\Sigma T/\Sigma C_d$, which is the rate of generation of output per unit of utilised costs, or cost of occupied facilities multiplied by the system's operating costs C_s:

$$C_s \times \Sigma T/\Sigma C_d = T_{pot} \tag{2.7}$$

The ratio T/T_{pot} which is the actual total earnings divided by the total earnings potential, can be shown to be equal to the conversion system productivity $\Sigma C_d/C_s$ and it cannot exceed unity. The rate that product conversion costs C_d, add value to materials is the primary product productivity index T/C_d, since it relates the unit output of products to their product conversion and facilities occupancy costs. The rate that systems costs C_s, are utilised and the total facilities occupied in adding value to throughput materials is a system facilities, or conversion utilisation index $\Sigma C_d/C_s$.

From these two major measures of systems productivity (the all product total earnings productivity and the conversion systems facilities productivity), the systems total earnings productivity is determined as:

$$\frac{\Sigma T}{\Sigma C_d} \times \frac{\Sigma C_d}{C_s} = \frac{\Sigma T}{C_s} \qquad (2.8)$$

This primary system's productivity index is the rate of generated systems total earnings per unit of systems facilities costs.

In order to maximise total earnings we must maximise the rate of generating these earnings. Theoretically this can be done by producing the optimum mix of products having high total earnings productivity indices on facilities and conversion resources which thereby are utilised to their optimum, or maximum, feasible capacity.

These productivity indices are developed quite readily from data available in the books of account maintained normally by most enterprises, provided product costs do not include any element of the costs of idle product processing facilities. The primary index—Total Earnings Productivity—has the convenient characteristic that it reveals the profitability, because an index of unity indicates a breakeven condition with no profit or loss. This leads to a secondary index—Profit Productivity—which aptly indicates profit for positive values and loss for negative values. The value itself is the rate of profit (or loss) per unit of processing cost.

2.3 COST CATEGORIES AND RELATIONSHIPS

The cost of operating an industrial-commercial system C_s, may be broken down in several ways. Increasingly, the per period costs of operating a modern industrial enterprise are becoming more fixed (or unavoidable) once the decision is taken to operate the enterprise and these costs tend to remain fixed over a wide range of systems outputs. Nevertheless, a part of the system's operating costs may be variable C_v, (and this plus the materials cost M, comprises the systems variable expenses V). The system's global factor cost F_s, equals the systems cost C_s, plus the materials cost M.

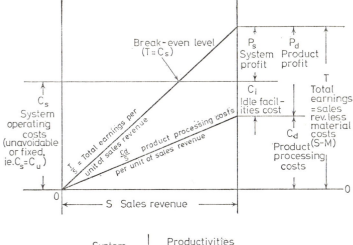

System	Productivities	
level	Total earnings	Profit
Product system	$\dfrac{\Sigma\,I}{\Sigma\,C_d}$	$\dfrac{\Sigma P_d}{\Sigma\,\overline{C_d}}$
Total system	$\dfrac{\Sigma\,I}{C_s}$	$\dfrac{P_s}{C_s}$

System safety factor $= \dfrac{P_s}{C_s + P_s}$ ($=\%$ reduction in T for T to equal C_s i.e. for system output to be reduced to a break even level.)

Note: $\dfrac{T - C_d}{S} = \dfrac{P_d}{S} = $ Product profitability.

Figure 2.1. Total Earnings—Sales Revenue (Break Even) Chart (all systems operating costs unavoidable or fixed per period—excluding materials costs within normal operating range)

While the unavoidable costs C_u, are incurred in providing, controlling and servicing the production capacity, part of these facilities normally are idle thereby incurring idle facilities costs C_i. The costs for the utilised part of the fixed facilities C_f, plus the variable processing cost C_v, equal the product cost C_d.

The idle facilities cost C_i, plus the utilised fixed facilities cost C_f, plus the variable processing cost C_v, equals the total systems cost C_s. These relationships are shown as follows:

$$C_i + C_f = C_u$$

$$C_f + C_v = C_d$$

$$C_u + C_v = C_s$$

$$C_d + C_i = C_s$$

$$M + C_v = V$$

$$M + C_s = F_s$$

When desirable, inventory costs C_{inv}, may be isolated from the active production system as may administrative costs C_{adm}, marketing costs C_{mkt}, production costs C_{prd} and:

$$C_{inv} + C_{adm} + C_{mkt} + C_{prd} = C_s \qquad (2.9)$$

When the variable processing costs C_v, approach zero, as they tend to do within the normal range of system outputs in many modern enterprises, the fixed facilities costs C_f, will approach the product costs C_d; the unavoidable costs C_u, will approach the systems costs C_s and the fixed facilities utilisation productivity

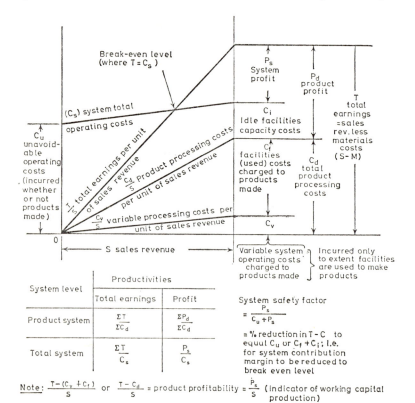

Figure 2.2 Total Earnings—Sales Revenue (Variable Break Even) Chart (system operating expenses mostly unavoidable—or fixed per period, but partly avoidable—or variable per period i.e. fixed per product)

C_f/C_v will approach the total facilities utilisation productivity, C_d/C_s.

In a system where the variable costs (excluding materials) are practically non-existent the pertinent cost (and revenue) categories for productivity costing purposes would be:

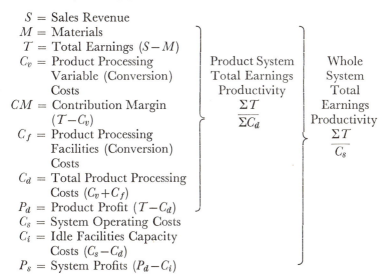

S = Sales Revenue
M = Materials Cost
T = Total Earnings $(S-M)$
C_d or C_f = Product Processing
P_d = Product Profit $(T-C_d)$
C_s = System Operating Costs
C_i = Idle Facilities Capacity Costs (C_s-C_d)
P = System Profit (P_d-C_i)

Product System Total Earnings Productivity $\dfrac{\Sigma T}{\Sigma C_d}$ or $\dfrac{\Sigma T}{\Sigma C_f}$

Whole System Total Earnings Productivity $\dfrac{\Sigma T}{C_s}$ or $\dfrac{\Sigma T}{C_u}$

The relationship between these cost-revenue categories is shown in Figure 2.1.

In a system where variable processing costs are significant a productivity costing group of cost-revenue categories would be:

S = Sales Revenue
M = Materials
T = Total Earnings $(S-M)$
C_v = Product Processing Variable (Conversion) Costs
CM = Contribution Margin $(T-C_v)$
C_f = Product Processing Facilities (Conversion) Costs
C_d = Total Product Processing Costs (C_v+C_f)
P_d = Product Profit $(T-C_d)$
C_s = System Operating Costs
C_i = Idle Facilities Capacity Costs (C_s-C_d)
P_s = System Profits (P_d-C_i)

Product System Total Earnings Productivity $\dfrac{\Sigma T}{\Sigma C_d}$

Whole System Total Earnings Productivity $\dfrac{\Sigma T}{C_s}$

The relationship between these cost-revenue categories is shown in Figure 2.2.

It is important to note that in productivity costing models, the product system excludes the costs of idle facilities capacity C_i. If these are subtracted from the product profit P_d, then the system profit P_s is derived.

Table 2.1 PRODUCTIVITY COSTING (PRODUCT) OPERATING STATEMENT

Product Item		A	B	C	D	Total
S Sales revenue	£	300 000	500 000	200 000	400 000	1 400 000
M Materials	£	50 000	400 000	100 000	150 000	700 000
T Total earnings	£	250 000	100 000	100 000	250 000	700 000
C_d Product Costs	£	200 000	60 000	50 000	100 000	410 000
P_d Product Profits	£	50 000	40 000	50 000	150 000	290 000
C_i Idle Capacity Costs	£	—	—	—	—	190 000
C_s Systems Costs	£	—	—	—	—	600 000
P_s Systems Profit	£	—	—	—	—	100 000
$\dfrac{T}{S}$ ratio		0·833	0·200	0·500	0·625	0·500
$\dfrac{T}{C_d}$ Total Earnings Product Productivity		1·250	1·667	2·000	2·500	1·708
$\dfrac{T}{C_s}$ Total Earnings Systems Productivity		—	—	—	—	1·167
$\dfrac{T}{S}$ ranking		1	4	3	2	—
$\dfrac{T}{C_d}$ ranking		4	3	2	1	—

As productivity costing removes the distorting effect of idle capacity from product preference criteria, it is useful in developing divisional and product operating statements. Table 2.1 shows such a statement developed from representative data of an electrical engineering company. Note that product A which has the highest total earnings sales ratio (0.833) also has the lowest total earnings product productivity (1.250).

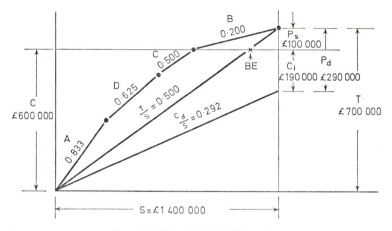

Figure 2.3. Hip Roof Profit-Volume chart

Based on Table 2.1 a Profit-Volume Hip-Roof Chart shown in Figure 2.3 may be developed. The Hip is the ordinary total systems total earnings-sales revenue vector, while the Roof represents the cumulative vectors of the positively ranked product total earnings-sales revenue ratios.

Chapter 3

Economists' Measures of Productivity

Most economists use indicators that are macro in nature, that is they study whole economies rather than activities at plant level. Labour time methods of measurement (hour, day, or year) are often used, the principle being to convert all input factors to labour time. This is based on concepts dating back to Adam Smith and Karl Marx.[15] They postulate that labour is the only source of value and it alone can transmute base materials into saleable products. All materials, depreciation, services and final products consisting of materialised labour can be converted into manpower equivalents by dividing the output, or input, in financial terms by the current average annual wages.

In 1949 Smith and Beeching[16] put forward proposals to reduce all inputs to labour inputs. They suggested that to labour used in a plant should be added the manpower equivalents of capital equipment, services, and materials bought. These additions to be estimated by taking the raw materials value, services and plant depreciation and dividing them by the national average annual income per employee. Thus there ends up a total number of 'men' that can be divided into the output for the year to get a figure of 'output per man-year':

i.e.

$$\frac{\text{Sales Output}}{\text{Total no. of Employees} + \left[\dfrac{\text{Capital} + \text{External Expenses}}{\text{Average Earnings per Annum}}\right]}$$

or

$$\frac{\text{Sales Output}}{\text{Labour (live)} + \text{Labour (Materialised)}}$$

In any event, the manpower equivalents using national averages are insufficiently refined for meaningful indices, while the exercise of obtaining them involves hazardous estimations. Easterfield[17] is aware of this in his criticism.

Another, and still more important weakness of the index is that sales figures are often quite misleading since they include bought-out materials, supplies and services, the price of which includes the profits of supplying companies. To overcome this, some economists, including those of the Department of Trade and Industry tend to use 'Net Output (or Added Value) per Employee' as a measure of productivity.

$$\text{Net Output per Employee} = \frac{\text{Added Value per Annum}}{\text{Total Number of Employees}}$$

$$= \frac{AV}{Ly} \qquad (3.1)$$

where: AV represents the value added to materials by the process of production and constitutes the fund from which wages, salaries, rent, rates, tax reserves and dividends, selling, distribution and advertising costs, have to be met as well as depreciation on machines, plant and buildings.

Added Value is obtained by subtracting the external expenses X from the total sales S value:

$$AV = S - X \qquad (3.2)$$

S is the total value of sales and work done + value of stocks at end of year adjusted for stocks held at the beginning of the year. X is the sum of external expenses: materials + contract service + power, fuel and water + packing and supplies + consumable items and tools. The external expenses however do not include capital expenditure which is consumed, or depreciated, over a period greater than one financial year. The total number of employees Ly is obtained by adding to the operatives Lo all other employees Ls both in units of man-years. Hence:

$$Ly = Lo + Ls \qquad (3.3)$$

where Lo represents those employed controlling machines and processes, in power houses, transport, stores, warehouses, canteens, inspection, maintenance and cleaning and all manual wage earners other than persons employed by the firm who work on materials supplied by the firm in their own homes. Ls represents the administrative, technical and clerical employees, including managers, superintendents, foremen, researchers, experimentalists, development engineers, design people, computer personnel, draughtsmen, tracers, representatives, salesmen, and all other office staff including executives and directors, other than those paid by fee only. Hence:

$$\frac{AV}{Ly} = \frac{S-X}{Lo+Ls} \qquad (3.4)$$

The influence that external expenses (materials and outside purchases) might have on this index have been expressly excluded therefore ensuring a slightly more consistent productivity measure than that of the accountant or the earlier economist measure. However, there are weaknesses and it must be treated with caution for it depends upon factors that are influenced by outside conditions and it would be easy to draw wrong conclusions.

The total number of employees $Lo+Ls$ needs to be examined carefully as only a percentage of operatives is directly related to productive processing and it is sensitive to changes of production methods and trade. No adjustment is made for the number who work part-time. For instance female labour is predominantly part-time and there is a proportionally high number employed nationally. Most are likely to be found in low capital areas doing light work or carrying out dexterous inspection and packing processes. We would suggest that 'man-hours worked' might be a more meaningful unit rather than numbers employed.

Lomax[14] suggests that mechanisation influences the proportion of operatives, 'direct' and 'indirect' and it is generally accepted that as a process becomes more automatic, more administrative and technical personnel are needed. However Melman,[18] as a result of research carried out at Standard Motors in 1955 considers that large highly mechanised plants can be operated at a high level of productivity with the application of management techniques that are simple, inexpensive and do not necessarily require a higher proportion of administrative and technical support.

Whatever the major cause, and in agreement with Lomax,[14] comparisons of operative/staff ratios indicate that the activities of operatives in manufacturing industries are changing to more of an administrative and technical nature. Perhaps, and in sympathy with Melman, company executives are unaware of the benefits, or may be incapable of applying modern managerial practices.

3.1 CENSUS OF PRODUCTION

Industries are classified by the Department of Trade and Industry[19] according to the nature of their activity and defined in terms of principle products appropriately placed under a Standard Industrial Classification order S.I.C.[20] This order corresponds fairly closely with that of the International Standard Industrial Classification I.S.I.C.[21] The S.I.C. order is further subdivided into minimum list headings m.l.h. in order to define more closely the product group. Appendix B lists these groupings. The census form is so constructed that operating ratios for such information as: employee numbers, net output per employee, net output as a proportion of sales, new investment per employee, average wages and salaries and operative/staff ratios can be determined so that individual companies can compare themselves to S.I.C. group averages both nationally and regionally.

In the West Midlands regional study[22] it was remarkable to find that few company executives and managements had knowledge of their company's S.I.C. and m.l.h. groups. Their company performances were found to be compared with competitors based on what was known about the competitor, and there appeared to be little interest in comparing formally their own performances with those of similar companies having similar activities, on a national or regional basis.

Inevitably errors in placing establishments into appropriate principal product groups do occur, and two very similar electrical companies (defined under electrical machinery by the S.I.C. in the Census of Production), have been found under different minimum list headings. Other similar principal product firms are also considered to be wrongly identified and listed. The West Midlands regional study suggests that the classification used by the census is not discriminating enough and points to the influence of labour intensive and capital intensive manufacturing activities.

Wrong identification was considered to be the result of a 'rule of exception' implemented by the Board of Trade in order to maintain comparisons between industrial groups in the censuses 1954, 1958 and 1963. This rule applies to establishments that were placed under an appropriate minimum list heading in 1954, and explains that an establishment would not be moved to another group in 1958 or 1963, unless the output of the new principal product increased by more than one third that of the old principal product. The principal products of the firms where listing errors have been found, however, have not changed since their inception.

From what has been said, it is understandable that most industrialists look upon the Census of Production as a burden which contributes nothing to a company's well being. They feel it would be hazardous to compare companies that are unique and heterogeneous and that such comparisons would be misleading.

3.2 CAPITAL CHARGES

To be constructive it might be more acceptable to have interim data analysed, published and possibly circulated to all participating companies. Furthermore, with a little extra effort, much more useful information could be extracted and developed into meaningful productivity since as Easterfield[23] points out: 'the current "net output per employee" statistics wrap up so many things in one parcel that they can hardly be used for prediction, or target setting, or analysis of factors affecting productivity, or drawing attention to particularly interesting plants, products or industries'.

Since this indicator does not take current capital employed into account it is likely to be more misleading, not only for interfirm comparisons, but also for regional and national comparisons. To correct some of the anomalies it would be reasonable to include in the 'inputs' the depreciation or capital charges. One such method of doing this would be to add the depreciation on a 'written down' replacement value to the total salaries and wages bill, (as is done in the Central Statistical Office 'Blue-Book' of National Income and Expenditure).[24]

i.e.
$$\frac{\text{Net Output (or Added Value) per annum}}{\text{Total Wages, Salaries and Benefits} + \text{Depreciation}}$$

In this method since the inputs have been converted into financial measures, both inputs and outputs are now in the same units.

An alternative method would be to extend the input by adding to the number of employees (adjusted for part-time employees) the capital charges which could be converted into their manpower equivalents, by treating the depreciation on a 'written down' replacement value, and to divide this by the national average annual income, thus ending up with an input of 'men'.

i.e.
$$\frac{\text{Net Output (or Added Value) per annum}}{\text{Adj. No. of Employees} + \left[\dfrac{\text{Adj. Depreciation}}{\text{National average annual income}}\right]}$$

As industry becomes more capital intensive it is capital rather than (or in conjunction with) labour that generates value. In such a model labour L, could be deducted as a throughput leaving capital cost K, as the sole input. The output would then be $AV - L = G$ or capital earnings. If a surplus of revenue from the sale of a productive system's products remains after personnel earnings L, for any given period have been met, probably the next most important demand on the system's revenue is to pay for the basic materials and supplies X, used in making the products. Any surplus revenue remaining is normally used first to liquidate other financial commitments incurred in operating the system, such as interest on borrowed funds, taxes on capital assets, liability insurances and capital equipment depreciation reserves K. Thereafter any surplus remaining is the system's operating profit for the period. In this scale, capital charges appear just before profits and after labour. It may therefore be possible to treat labour, like materials, as a throughput. The capital charges productivity then becomes:

$$\frac{K+P}{K} = \frac{G}{K} \tag{3.5}$$

The determination of the actual division of the total earnings or added value generated between personnel L, and capital K, is difficult to achieve. If the expected return on capital charges employed is provided for as the equivalent of wages and salaries being the return to labour, it may be claimed that part of the residual profit (after providing for required return on capital) is generated by both labour and capital. If this is so then the added value generated by labour, which includes management, would be AV_l, and the added value generated by capital charges would be AV_a, where:

$$AV_l + AV_a = AV \tag{3.6}$$

The residual profit generated by the two parts of added value could be derived by subtracting the labour L, or capital K, from their respective added value contributions; i.e.

$$AV_a - L = P_l \tag{3.7}$$

and

$$AV_a - K = P_a \tag{3.8}$$

This could be a possible method of added value or profit sharing between labour and capital, and could be the basis of improved productivity bargaining and incentive schemes.

Many conventional measures are based on partial productivity indices[25] Total Output/Single Input. A partial productivity index of capital charges would be AV/K but this ignores labour L, which is included in the AV or $L+K+P$, but not in the capital charge K. The deduction of labour from the added value to bring it into line with the denominator may provide a more efficient capital charge productivity index. Nevertheless it is difficult to justify the conceptual equivalent for capital earnings $G = K+P$, that one has

c

24

for human earnings $L+P = H$. Figure 3.1 shows the relation of capital charge earnings to the human earnings H, model. Then the capital charges profitability is P/K. Note that TP refers to the conceptual systems throughput.

Capital can be divided between fixed and circulating capital, the fixed being mainly in equipment, building and land and the circulating consisting mainly of materials stocks, work-in-progress, finished stocks, and ready money. The capital charges for the fixed capital are based on applying the capital recovery factor related to the expected life of the plant and to the replacement cost of the assets.

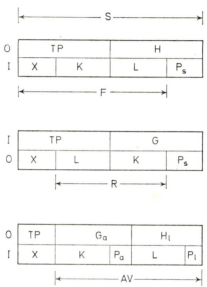

Figure 3.1. *Labour-Capital Productivity Models*

Regarding working capital, its charges are based on applying the standard interest rate to the stocks, work-in-progress and cash assets, including interest actually paid and bank charges. Cost of rented plant and land (alternative costs) can be treated with the capital costs, since the choice between paying interest or rental is merely a question of business expediency.[26]

A problem arises as to the treatment of interest as an imputed charge which has not actually been paid. The main reason for inclusion of interest as a capital charge is that bringing accountancy into line with economic concepts of cost, develops an improved basis of management decision making and productivity measurement. If however these imputed costs are included, an equivalent imputed income should be included with revenue. These imputed costs and revenues can be excluded for national accounting purposes.

3.3 INTERNATIONAL COMPARISONS

In international comparisons it is generally acknowledged that output per head is two-and-a-half times greater in certain American industries than that of comparable industries in Britain. Catherwood cited by Jones and Barnes[3] gave such a comparison for the Aluminium industry and suggested that it must be true for other industries as well. Numerous comparisons have since been made,

Table 3.1 COMPARISON OF U.S.A. AND U.K. ELECTRICAL AND ELECTRONIC FIRMS

| | Base Sales a 100 units | | | |
	U.S. Companies		U.K. Companies	
Sales	100·0		100·0	
Profits before Tax and Loan interest	10·0		9·0	
	Equivalent Month's/Annual		*Equivalent Month's/Annual*	
	Sales	*Sales*	*Sales*	*Sales*
Capital Employed				
Fixed Capital				
Operating Assets	2·0	17·0	2·8	23·0
Investments and other fixed assets	0·4	3·0	0·8	7·0
	2·4	20·0	3·6	30·0
Working Capital				
Inventories	2·2	18·0	4·3	36·0
Debtors and repayments	2·0	17·0	4·1	34·0
Creditors and accruals (Deduct)	(1·8)	(15·0)	(2·4)	(20·0)
	2·4	20·0	6·0	50·0
Total Capital Employed	4·8	40·0	9·6	80·0
Profit to Sales	10·0%		9·0%	
Ratio Sales to Capital Employed	2·5		1·25	
Profit to Capital Employed	25·0%		11·25%	
Sales per £1 or Fixed operating assets	£5·9		£4·4	
Sales per employee (£1 = $2·80)	£6 000		£2 700	

the most recent one comparing output per head in the British Aircraft industry with the American Aircraft industry. The conclusion was that two-and-a-half men are needed to produce the same output as one man employed in a comparable American industry.

Such observations are shrugged aside by some British industrialists who regard comparisons as misleading, especially when official statistics of investment and degree of mechanisation often show British industry as the poor relation. The natural reaction is to assume that an American worker and certain European workers have a higher degree of mechanisation and capital intensity than an equivalent British worker.

However, the report[27] on a recent study of comparable electrical and electronic firms in the U.S.A. and U.K., summarised in Table 3.1 indicates that the ratio of sales to fixed capital assets was 50% higher in the U.S.A. than in the U.K. The report concludes that an American company of comparable size would have no more equipment and facilities than its counterpart in this country, but by better utilisation of these assets and manpower would obtain a much higher sales output.

It is pertinent to note also that the working capital requirements in the U.K. at 50% sales was two-and-a-half times that of the American companies at 20% sales. The report states that the rate of turnover of inventories in the U.S.A. is approximately double that in this country and this factor probably more than any other contributes to their higher turnover of total capital employed. Most important perhaps the sales per employee in the U.S.A. at £6 000 were more than double the £2 700 per employee in the U.K.

The return on capital employed in the U.S.A. was also more than double at 0.25 or 25% the 11.25% return achieved in the U.K. A much higher rate of turnover of working capital and equipment in the U.S.A. are unquestionably the main reasons for these large differentials.

In the interests of the British economy and in order to maximise the return on capital invested, machine utilisation must be regarded as important as labour utilisations. Risk[28] writes: 'Check the utilisation of every expensive piece of plant and machinery, squeeze more production or service from it . . . make sure that you use your capital effectively'.

Chapter 4

Engineers' Measures of Productivity

Productivity and Efficiency are often regarded as synonymous.
Engineers speak of efficiency (Eff) as the measure of the amount of
energy (fuel) supplied (If) and converted into useful work (Ou)

$$Eff = \frac{Ou}{If} \leqslant 1$$

Productivity (Pro) as defined by the 'Terminology of Productivity'[29] is the quotient obtained by dividing product output (Ou)
by one of the factors of production (If) whether it be capital,
investment, or raw material. Hence:

$$Pro = \frac{Ou}{If} = Eff \leqslant 1 \qquad (4.1)$$

Bahiri and Martin[30] consider, and most engineers have the same
view, that productivity is related to the efficiency of the producing
activity and therefore implies an output/input relationship. As
such it is a version of the normal engineering expression for the
efficiency of a machine. The input may be said to generate the
output. Since the input is converted to the output it cannot exceed
unity in the physical sense but may do so in financial values. Also
since the potential output is equal to the input the degree of achievement of this conversion (useful/potential), is another measure of
efficiency that cannot exceed unity.

When we conceive of outputs being generated by inputs it is
obvious that the useful output cannot be more than input, so it
can never have an index greater than unity. In financial terms
however, the value of outputs must be greater than the cost of
inputs if the business is to make a profit.

27

For useful output (Ou) to reach its potential useful output (Op) depends upon how well the input factor (If) is utilised:
Hence:

$$\text{Pro} = \frac{Ou}{If} = \frac{If - Losses}{If} = \frac{Ou}{Op} = \text{Eff} \leqslant 1 \qquad (4.2)$$

From this expression we have three productivity efficiency ratios:

(1) Generation of useful output by input—useful output/input
(2) Utilisation of systems input—effective input/actual input
(3) Actual (useful) output to Potential (useful) output—actual output/potential output

Utilisation of resources compared to a standard, such as producing more from a given combination of input factors, or a given useful output from less inputs, is regarded as the improvement of productivity, and a low utilisation of input factors as low productivity. Consequently we define and measure relative productivity levels in comparison with a level achieved in the past or in comparison with another establishment in the same industry, or in comparison with the national average achieved by another nation.

4.1 STANDARDS OF EFFICIENCY

Since it has been said that only the utilised parts of labour and machines add value to the manufacture of products, then the efficiency with which value is added should be measured. For the engineer this measurement depends upon the concept of a standard against which the efficiency can be compared.

Work Measurement supported by Method Study provides useful standards, but have a built in component of judgement aggravated by policies of wage payment. The means of establishing these standards varies considerably between industries and between firms within given industries.

'A standard obtained by measuring inappropriate methods of working is no standard. Equally, a standard obtained by timing one man on one job is not a standard, only a source of argument. Thus it is essential that an acceptable method is devised before work measurement studies are taken and that several operatives (representative of those doing the same standardised job) are timed in a proper manner before a standard is presented'.[31]

Before Taylor and Gilbreth developed their analytical techniques of time and motion study, payment by results was determined, and still is determined in many companies, by ratefixers who base their standards of efficiency on extracts from past records, experience, manufacturers' tables, or by stop-watch timing. The ratefixer generally confines his methods examination to tooling layouts, machine feeds and speeds and product specifications outlined on the operation planning sheet. Before the time is accepted as the rate for the job, bargaining at shop floor level is carried out as an accepted practice between the operative, ratefixer, foreman, and on occasions the shop steward. Shimmin[32] writes:

'Both the ratefixer and the operative know that the final value for the job will bear little or no relationship to the time it actually takes. The ratefixer, with tongue in cheek, not only expects but is prepared to climb down in bargaining. Ultimately, both settle for some value between extremes which by the nature of the compromise will be a potential source of trouble and dispute in the future'.

Many trade union officials consider that a rate fixed system has an in built opportunity for bargaining which favours shop floor workers simply because it enables them to participate in setting their own earnings levels.[33]

Nevertheless a measurement system that depends almost entirely on mutual agreement provides little opportunity for management and workers to compare the effectiveness of their work with that of a representative standard. The measure of success in any working situation is performance against a standard and in applying work study techniques it is important to realise that there are very few short cuts and none for the beginner.

4.2 STANDARD TIME

Time Study, according to Dudley[34] cannot be regarded as an isolated and self contained tool of management (as ratefixing tends to be), but must be viewed as one of several complementary techniques collectively known as Work Study. Thus before time study is carried out the observer must see that two basic conditions have been satisfied:

(1) the operation has been standardised
(2) the task is being performed in the approved manner by a trained and experienced operative

Dudley[35] also points out that this standardisation of the layout and method of working will normally have resulted from a systematic method or motion study during which the causes of fatigue will have been eliminated wherever possible. Careful selection of the worker ensures that the work is within his physical and mental capacity and yet makes reasonable demands on him. Training and experience will further reduce the likelihood of abnormal fatigue.

The procedure for establishing Standard Time, outlined by Norman[36] can be illustrated simply as shown in Figure 4.1 (page 32) where the shaded rectangle in each block represents a percentage of the appropriate term added to the said term.

Taylor[37] laid down what is still recognised as a primary step in the preparation for a time study that each job should be carefully subdivided into elementary operations and should receive the most thorough time study. An element is a distinct part of a job usually consisting of a number of basic movements (therblig groups) which need to be identified in order to recognise the method used and conveniently arranged for:

(1) observation
(2) measurement
(3) extension
(4) analysis

However inconsistency persists between time-study observers in their element selection and make up. They tend to be individualistic in the choice of breakpoints (the instant at which one element ends and another begins). A job might consist of eight types of element and their relationship may be shown as follows:

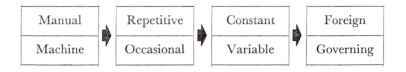

This suggests that elements can either be:

Manual repetitive and constant, or
Machine repetitive and constant, or
Manual repetitive and variable, or
Machine repetitive and variable, or
Manual occasional and constant, or
Machine occasional and constant, and so on.

In order to retain some consistency in element selection, Currie[38] advocates elements of between 10 and 50 centiminutes duration realising that there is a limit below which accuracy can be maintained in reading a stop watch and also in recognising that elements of work can be strongly influenced by the rate of working and effort required.

To assess the speed, effort and effectiveness put into each element of work a practitioner compares the operative's rate of work with that of a 'trained' concept of standard rate expressed by means of numbers in accordance with a rating scale:

Bedeaux 60/80	Metric 100/133	B.S.3138 0/100	
—100	—166	—125	—*Very fast:* operative exhibits a high degree of assurance.
—80	—133	—100	—*Brisk:* incentive performance working with zest and interest. An operative of average ability and attainment who is motivated.
—60	—100	—75	—*Unhurried:* non incentive performance. Working steady and deliberate.
—40	—67	—50	—*Very slow:* operative appears half asleep having no interest in job. Time being intentionally wasted.
—0	—0	—0	—*Stopped* condition.

B.S.3138[39] recommends the 0/100 rating scale (where 100 corresponds to 80 and 133 on the 60/80 (Bedeaux) and 100/133 (Metric) scales respectively) and explains that standard rate should not be the supposed rating of a 'timeworker' (i.e. daywork, identified by the lower points of 60 and 100 on the other scales), but the rating to be expected from a worker of average ability and attainment who is motivated to apply himself to his work. Referring to the B.S. rating scale, Graham[40] points out that only two working speeds have a special meaning—0 which is the stopped condition and 100 which is the standard motivated condition. All other speeds are only relative to those two reference points.

Rating, according to Barnes[41] is a matter of judgement on the part of a time study engineer, and in support Marriott[42] recognises it as: 'probably the most difficult part of time-study mainly because it is entirely subjective and a matter of the observer relying entirely on his judgement.

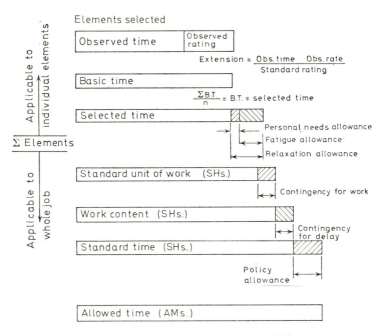

Figure 4.1. Procedure for Establishing Standard Time

The number of work cycles through which any particular element of activity should be observed varies directly as the amount of variation in the basic times of the elements. If work study practitioners maintain rating concepts and keep to orthodox procedure then consistency might be controlled even to the point of eliminating the variations. Matthew[43] found that where groups of time study engineers were trained on established standards of performance they could achieve surprising results within certain limits of accuracy and consistency. Given the right methods, selection and training of work study men Currie[38] agrees that such variations could be minimised.

Research indicates that there is some interdependence and interaction between rating and relaxation allowances. Dudley[35] states: 'although rating is merely an assessment of actual working pace relative to the establishment of standard pace, it also involves the consideration of effort or skill demanded by the nature of the operation. . . . Hence in the process of rating . . . allowances are made for the fact that some jobs are more fatiguing than others and C.R. allowances (relaxation allowance) also graded according to effort, are additional to these'. An operative's working pace can be affected by: attention required, concentration, confined working space, abnormal working conditions, special clothing, and these obviously present an element of inconsistency in assessing the actual working pace relative to standard rate.

The rating assessment is not intended to provide allowances to overcome periods of exertion. Relaxation allowances are judged necessary to compensate for this. A personal needs allowance is generally accepted as constant within a working group, or situation, and as observed by Dudley is a form of relaxation that is, 'under the worker's control and tends to be grouped towards the beginning and end of each working period'. Fatigue allowance, although the causes will have been eliminated wherever possible, is one where judgement is most vulnerable. Murrell[44] explains that 'rest point cannot be determined objectively because it takes some time for lactic acid to accumulate and give a subjective sense of fatigue'.

To add further to the ambiguities that arise in the procedure towards Standard Time an additional allowance known as Policy Allowance is often provided to make the earnings level more attractive. The I.Prod.E. and I.C.W.A.[45] found that: 'This wage policy allowance was variable within each firm . . . and introduced to the rate as padding. . . . In fact in the majority of firms, time study rates are not used as standards of measurement but as means of bolstering up a basic hourly wage to an attractive level'. The addition of this allowance to Standard Time SM_s, changes the unit of value to Allowed Time expressed in allowed minutes AM_s, and it has been shown by Lupton[46] that this addition is often bargained for at shop floor level between the time study man and the operative, a practice that is identical to that of ratefixing.

In addition to measuring labour performance against some pre-determined standard Nadler[47] suggests that there are several levels (or standards) that may be compared, the highest being the theoretical ideal system. This is a measure of efficiency and/or effectiveness since an actual or designed system is being compared to a potential one.

An interesting method that combines a potential or ideal concept with standard indices is being used in a large electrical company in the Midlands. The method makes use of a technical index which is equal to the minimum work time under conditions of large scale rationalisation of product design and improved methods. This index is multiplied by a labour utilisation index which is the standard time divided by the actual time taken, and the productivity index obtained:

Productivity index = Technical index × Labour utilisation index

or $\quad \dfrac{\text{Ideal Time}}{\text{Actual Time}} = \dfrac{\text{Ideal Time}}{\text{Standard Time}} \times \dfrac{\text{Standard Time}}{\text{Actual Time}}$ $\quad$ (4.3)

This is similar to the concept advocated in productivity costing[30] to measure ratios of productive work costs to standard product conversion costs and total system costs, i.e.

$$\frac{C_e}{C_s} = \frac{C_e}{C_d} \times \frac{C_d}{C_s} \qquad (4.4)$$

where C_e = Cost of productive work, C_d = Standard facilities occupancy cost, C_s = Standard system cost (including idle capacity C_i).

The above indices represent a method of converting facilities productive time measures into their cost equivalents. For the method (Technical index × Labour utilisation) it is also possible to convert these time inputs to cost inputs.

4.3 PERFORMANCE INDICES

Schemes based on work measurement principles provide a measure of performance against a standard by which both management and workers compare the effectiveness of their work, the basis of which is an operator or Group Performance index:

$$\frac{\text{Standard time for work done (measured)}}{\text{Actual time taken to do the work}} \times 100$$

The standard time for a job is the sum of clock times required by a qualified workman to:

(1) carry out his task at the standard level of performance
(2) recover from the physical and mental strains imposed by his task
(3) compensate him for small contingent delays which are likely to occur in his working day and for which management are responsible

Table 4.1 OVERALL WORK'S PERFORMANCES

Department	Attendance Time	Time on Unmeasured Work	Attendance Time on Measured Work	Standard Minutes or Hours Available	Performance Index
	X	Y	B	A	$\%$
	From Clock Cards and Registers	From Supervisor's Log or Job Cards	$(X-Y)$	From Job Cards, Register or planning sheets	$\dfrac{A}{B} \times 100$
Workshops Stores Maintenance Transport Administration etc.					

Overall Work's Performance index $\qquad \dfrac{\Sigma A}{\Sigma B} \times 100$

Performance indices are used to determine the effective use of labour. They are the means of establishing the performance of an operator or a group of operators, for the purpose of bonus payment and to assist in the decision and control of a working situation. There are two main indices used:

(1) operator performance
(2) departmental performance

Operator performance

$$= \frac{\text{Total credit of measured SM}_s}{\text{Input of man-minutes on measured work}} \times 100 \quad (4.5)$$

Departmental performance

$$= \frac{\text{Total measured SMs} + \text{Total unmeasured SM}_s}{\text{Total Clock Attendance time-minutes}} \times 100 \quad (4.6)$$

By tabulating all departmental performance indices (Table 4.1) a third index Overall Work's Performance, can be obtained:

Under incentive conditions, work to be carried out is normally costed and programmed on the basis of standard performance, i.e., a 100 performance equivalent to an operative working with zest and interest (regarded as incentive rate and 100 on the British Standard 0/100 rating scale) who takes his fully assessed relaxation allowance throughout a normal working period. This 100 performance is known as the Standard Operator Performance, whereas the performance an operator attains during a working period is known as the Actual Operator Performance.

The Standard Performance indices are useful in estimating the cost of a job and in programming future work. When work is in progress the comparison of Actual Performance with that of Standard Performance indicates whether estimated costs and programmed times are likely to be met.

Thus:

$$\frac{\text{Actual Departmental Performance}}{\text{Standard Departmental Performance}} \times 100$$

becomes a useful guide to labour performance levels and to the effectiveness of supervision.

4.4 OTHER PHYSICAL MEASURES

Other physical measures of utilisation and productivity that the engineer can call upon are:

(1) *Volume or quantity of output*

In homogeneous product type manufacture such as gas and electricity, the physical volume of output can be regarded as an absolute measure of productivity. However where there is a possibility of product or quality grading as found in coalmining and foundries, it may be difficult to compare physical units with sufficient reliability. In heterogeneous product type industries physical units of output present an even more difficult comparison.

Physical characteristics, specifications and price differ considerably in most manufacturing industries, and in such situations financial units could be more meaningful and reliable; observing that adjustments must be made for price inflation and changes, especially before any inter-firm comparisons are made.

(2) *Horse-power and electricity consumption*

There is a close correlation in many firms between horsepower and the new replacement cost of equipment, the reason being that as a facility increases in value there is often a corresponding increase in horsepower rating. While this linear relationship does not always hold true for all types of power equipment, non linear production functions can be developed which will cater for these. Where the relationship is reasonably linear a kilowatt hour can be converted to its equivalent labour hours via use of cost functions.

We may easily convert horsepower into equivalent kWh by multiplying by 0.746. For example, a departmental horsepower rating was 259 and if all the facilities were running during the entire hour then 193 kWh (259×0.746) would be consumed. Adjusting for lighting and other minor usages, an estimated usage potential of 200 kWh should be possible. If in any one hour 120 kWh electricity was consumed then the department would be 60% ($100 \times 120/200$) productive. Over a year the capacity would be 200 kWh $\times$ 4 000 potential working hours = 800 000 kWh against 480 000 kWh or 60% utilised.

A supplementary approach would be to compare the actual labour hours in a given period against the quantity that would be used if all the facilities were fully manned and operating. For example, if all the facilities were manned and running this would involve 220 000 man hours booked against jobs. Assuming only 165 000 man hours were booked then there would be a utilisation of 75% ($100 \times 165/100$).

If by relative weighting of total costs it was found that 1/3 expenses were due to labour and 2/3 incurred by facilities then these would be the relative weighting factors applied.

A combined index which takes the two factors into account would then be:

$$\left(\frac{480}{800} \times 0 \cdot 333\right) + \left(\frac{165}{220} \times 0 \cdot 667\right) = 0 \cdot 65 \text{ or } 65\% \text{ utilisation}$$

The use of engineering based short cut methods should aid in productivity measurement, cost apportionment, systems analysis and interfirm analyses.

Such physical measures as machine and space utilisations, materials and waste controls are all useful to the engineer, but whatever the measure or indices used, caution must be exercised before reliable conclusions can be drawn.

While being aware of the physical controls of input most engineers and/or production supervisors are not aware of the financial implications. A report[48] says: 'It may be uneconomic to seek the minimum expenditure in the use of manpower if this detracts from the optimum use of expensive capital equipment. The combination of capital and labour can be varied to give the same output.' If more capital is invested and labour reduced, or maintained at the same level, net output per employee might rise, but it does not necessarily indicate that the system is more productively applied, especially if it is found that the total unit costs have risen.

Chapter 5

Integrated Productivity Model

It is possible to develop an integrated productivity model with both outputs and inputs in financial units, and comprehensive enough to embrace various productivity concepts. Examination of Figure 5.1 in conjunction with the nomenclature lists of Tables 5.1 and 5.2 shows the integration of four models and their inter-relationships.

Starting from the accountant's total expense or global factor S/F (which corresponds to the total factor productivity as used by the French National Committee for Productivity),[49] the integrated model progresses by steps through the other three concepts by successively eliminating the non essential cost items from the models. These non essential items are the throughput investments or costs

Table 5.1 MAJOR SYSTEMS NOTATION

O = Output = $S = T = AV = H$
S = Sales Revenue or Gross Output
T = Total Earnings, Engineers Added Value or Conversion Output = $S-M$
AV = (Economists') Added Value or Net Output = $S-X$ or $T-C_x$
H = Net Earnings = $S-N$ or $AV-K$
I = Inputs = $F = C = R = L$
M = Materials Throughput
C_x = Indirect External Expenses
X = Total External Purchases = $M+C_x$
K = Capital Charges
N = Non-Labour Factorial Costs
L = Employment or Labour Charges
P = Profits = $O-I = S-F = T-L = AV-R = H-L$
R = Internal Expenses = $K+L$
C = Conversion Costs = $K+L+C_x$
F = Total Factorial Inputs = $X+K+L = S-P$
TP = Throughput or Investment Costs

D

39

Table 5.2 INTEGRATED SYSTEMS INDICES NOTATION

S/F = Global Factor Productivity or Gross Efficiency

T/C = Total Earnings Productivity or Conversion Efficiency

AV/R = Added Value Productivity

H/L = Net Added Value Labour Productivity

P/F = Total Factor Profit Productivity $= \dfrac{S}{F} - 1$

P/C = Conversion Profit Productivity $= \dfrac{T}{C} - 1$

P/R = Internal Profit Productivity $= \dfrac{AV}{R} - 1$

P/L = Labour Profit Productivity $= \dfrac{H}{L} - 1$

---

pertaining to each particular productivity concept. The measurement of productivity in each case is the rate of generation of output for that conceptual model per related unit of input.

For example, while the accountant's measure of global factor productivity would be S/F and the engineer's measure of conversion efficiency T/C, the economist's measures of added value and labour productivity would be AV/R and H/L. While reference is made to accountant's, engineer's or economist's models this reference only relates to the main conceptual emphases; all the models are in reality a synthesis of accounting, engineering and economic concepts.

One major advantage of this composite type model is that it is useful in converting the data from productivity research based on one particular concept into any of the other conceptual models. This facilitates integration of research work based on different conceptual productivity models.

Almost all the expenditures of an industrial-commercial system can be organised into the categories as shown in the block diagram Figure 5.1 namely, direct throughput materials M, indirect materials and externally purchased supplies and services C_x, which together with materials, make up the external expenses X. Depreciation, insurance, interest, rates and rents K, together with the external expenses X, make up the non personnel cost N. The personnel cost L, including wages, salaries, benefits and bonuses (plus those of management), together with the non personnel cost N, makes up the grand total or global cost F. Similarly, the internal operating expenses R, equals $L + K$, and the production conversion cost C, equals $L + K + C_x$.

Profits P, are the differences between these various expenditure levels and the related value of the output according to the particular productivity concept used, but adjusted for changes in value of assets. Taxes before profits, such as rates, are treated as inputs from other sectors, since government provides industries with other services. Rent and interest, would in the pure labour theory of

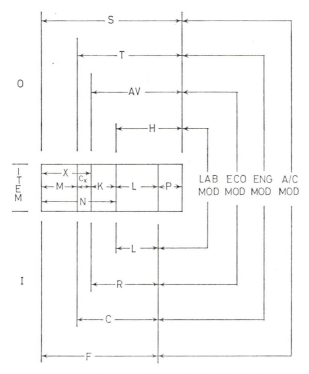

Figure 5.1. *Integrated Systems Productivity Model*

value, be included with profit as forms of surplus value rather than with inputs.

The measure of profit or profitability in each case is the profit (which is the same in all models) divided by the input criteria, P/F, P/C, P/R or P/L as the case may be. In all cases each is equivalent to the related systems generating productivity index, less unity, as has been shown previously for the relationship between T/C and P/C, according to productivity costing concepts.

In all models, only those resources utilised in generating output are productive, as shown in the generalised system productivity model Figure 5.2. The product profit is the pertinent output less the utilised input. This is the profit that would have been made if there were no non-product producing expenses.

The system profit is obtained by deducting from the product profit P_d, the non utilised or idle system inputs I_i. By substituting in Figure 5.2 the specific inputs for any one of the four systems

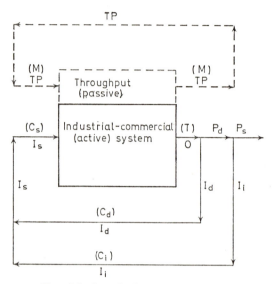

Figure 5.2. Generalised Productivity Model

productivity concept models, the specific model for that concept can be developed.

Measures of the utilisation of factors, resources or facilities I_d/I_s can be developed for all four conceptual systems. In the engineering model all operating expenses are allocated to the potentially productive facilities at which productive work may be done. The degree of utilisation or occupancy of these facilities in producing saleable products is another measure of the system's efficiency.

In so far as each type of cost or departmental expenditure is isolated and its utilisation evaluated a productivity index can be developed for that expenditure or category. It is possible to break-down the global systems costs into the following accounting or departmental categories; sales, distribution and marketing; adminis-tration; materials, inventory and storage; research, design and development; maintenance; materials processing (including such subclassifications as for materials, transportation and handling, plant layout, quality control and inspection). Expenses may also be subdivided by type of expenditure, such as for personnel, machinery, space, supplies and capital charges. Expenses incurred in one section but caused by inefficiency in another section can be allocated to the section responsible. Each factor can be measured separately to get its measure of (utilisation) productivity,

$$\frac{\text{minimum practical expenditure for present output level}}{\text{actual expenditure} + \text{losses due to factor efficiency}}$$

If all pertinent separate factors are combined, a measure of a system, or sub-system, productivity can be determined. In measuring administrative productivity, both use of manpower (evaluated by activity sampling and other work measurement methods) and of facilities (office machines and space-evaluated by sampling and direct measurement) require analysis and combination in terms of their cost accounting units. Similarly, the utilisation of manpower in whatever department or function it is occupied, can be analysed and evaluated. By evaluating each micro cost item separately it is possible to combine them in many ways since they are all determinable in terms of utilisation of cost inputs.

The added value (or net earnings) concept as a means of measuring productivity is favoured by many economists. The United States Bureau of Census and the British Census Authority follow this concept which is defined as the output of a firm, less materials, supplies, fuel, power and contracted work. Maverick[50] suggests that since production consists of adding value to the materials (in which he includes all short range outside purchases), the factor productivity index should be modified by subtracting or excluding these external expenses X, from both the numerator S, and denominator F. Thus the added value productivity is $S - X/F - X$ or AV/R which is the added value divided by the internal expenses.

The added value input/output analysis concept is often used in macro economic studies of both under developed economies and sector output of developed economies.[25] This is one of the more important purposes of the added value concept. For example, the import component of exports is the equivalent of the external expense X, incurred to enable the internal economic system R, to generate the value added AV, to these imports so that they can be exported for a sales income S. Very often the term 'value added' refers to value added by labour (or surplus value). In the Leontief[51] input-output analysis of macro sectors, capital purchases are included with outside purchases, so that in effect the output corresponds to H, or value added by labour L.

It is not necessary to use the added value productivity model in micro economic studies at plant level since it is similar in concept to the total earnings T, conversion model, but does not have the integrated cost accounting system advantages of the conversion model described. The total earnings, conversion, or engineers productivity model is therefore preferable for studies at plant level, except where comparisons of added value are required. For macro economic studies the advantages of the added value AV, productivity model are obvious and this is therefore the major area of its usefulness. It may also be preferable as a basis for comprehensive, plant-wide incentive schemes.[52]

Appendix A

Interfirm Comparisons for Management

H. INGHAM and L. TAYLOR HARRINGTON

The term *interfirm comparison* (IFC) refers to an organised pooling between firms of an industry of key business data on an anonymous, confidential and agreed uniform basis. Each company taking part (for an agreed fee) receives a confidential report showing *how* its overall success compares with that of others in the same industry, and *why* it differs from theirs. These reports are prepared with the needs of the Managing Director in mind: they evaluate his company's profit, cost, asset utilisation and physical performance ratios in the light of the results of his competitors; they alert him to those major aspects of policy and performance which require his special attention, and indicate the directions in which improvements should be made. In other words, IFC is not a statistical survey, but an important aid to self-diagnosis for each of the firms taking part. In conducting an IFC every care is taken to ensure that participants cannot be identified, and that the figures contributed are strictly comparable.

Among the organisations conducting such IFC for management is the Centre for Interfirm Comparison Ltd. with whose work the authors are closely associated. The Centre was set up in 1959 as an independent, autonomous and non profit making organisation by the British Institute of Management in association with the British Productivity Council in order to meet the demand of industry and trade for an expert body to conduct interfirm comparisons on a confidential basis as a service to management. Prior to the setting up of the Centre the authors, as members of staff of the British Institute of Management, were responsible for long term research (covering the practices of most European companies and the U.S.A.) into methods used in interfirm comparison, including the comparative measurement of productivity. However, the research did not only cover technical questions of measurement but also such matters of application as how to stimulate companies to take part in an IFC; how to present the data of the IFC in a way likely to raise interest at general management level and to secure its involvement, particularly as far as the implementation

45

of decisions taken to remedy weaknesses revealed by the IFC results were concerned.

So far, the Centre has prepared or conducted interfirm comparisons in some seventy industry and trades. Most of these comparisons were carried out in co-operation with the Trade Associations concerned.

Like the British Institute of Management, the Centre for Interfirm Comparison is concerned with the individual firm; its success, and the part played by general management in making it successful. It is the Centre's policy to ensure that the content of its interfirm comparisons appeals to those at general management level in participating firms because:

(1) the results of an IFC provide a stimulus to self criticism; if self criticism starts at the top, it will have the strongest impact on the development of the firm concerned.

(2) general management is in the best position to decide on remedial action, and to see to its implementation.

This means that an IFC will have the greatest impact if it deals with matters of concern to the men who are not primarily concerned with any one major function or department of the business, but who are responsible for ensuring that through proper co-ordination of the manufacturing, marketing, financial and other major operations of the business, a satisfactory profit is earned on the capital it employs.

A.1 Management Ratios

The concern with direction and control dictates the data—management ratios—to be covered in an IFC for general management. They will normally take as a starting point the ratio of

$$\frac{\text{Operating profit*}}{\text{Operating assets}}$$

This ratio reflects the earning power of a business and shows whether profitable use has been made of its assets. A favourable ratio helps the business to show a satisfactory return on shareholders' capital. It relates

* Operating profit is the profit (before tax) earned through the normal operations of the business; it excludes income from investments outside the business. Operating assets are (in manufacturing businesses): land and buildings, plant and machinery and other fixed assets plus stocks and debtors (investment outside the business is excluded).

In some comparisons conducted by the Centre, the ratio of net profit to equity capital is used as a primary ratio. The secondary ratios in such a scheme enable participants to consider, in addition to ratios showing the profitability of asset utilisation, such matters as capital gearing and interest paid on non-owners' capital. However, the bulk of the explanatory ratios covered by such a scheme will be the same as those shown in the *pyramid* diagram (Table A.1) since at least in manufacturing industries, differences between net profit/equity capital ratios of participating companies will be due largely to differences in their ratios of operating profit/operating assets.

Table A.1

(Courtesy of the Centre for Interfirm Comparison Ltd. 1970)

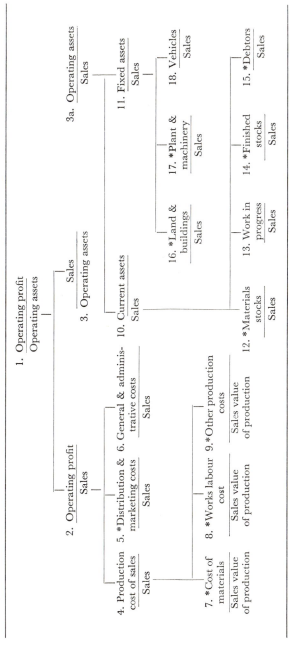

* Additional ratios and certain background data were provided to throw light on causes of differences in the asterisked ratios. These additional data are described in the Project Notes for the Light Engineering Scheme available on request from the Centre for Interfirm Comparison. For reasons of space the *depth pyramid* covering these additional data cannot be presented here; however, some of them are listed in section (4).

the assets used in normal activities to the profit derived from the employment of operating assets, and is the usual 'primary' ratio in an IFC for general management.

The other ratios covered by the IFC are selected to show in successive stages and in a systematic logical manner *why* the above mentioned primary ratio differs between firms. Since such a set of management ratios can be presented diagrammatically in the form of a pyramid it is now commonly called the *pyramid set of ratios*. The outline of such a set is reproduced in the following example which is given here to show how the management of a firm can benefit from taking part in an IFC.

A.2 An Example of Interfirm Comparison

The following is a much condensed example of an IFC in a light engineering industry. It is a hypothetical example, but based upon the kind of figures normally found in IFC's at the Centre. In the actual comparison about thirty-five firms took part. Some forty ratios with a considerable amount of background information were provided to participants.

(1) *Pyramid of Ratios*

The pyramid of ratios presented below shows the set of the major management ratios covered by the IFC and explains why the individual ratios were chosen.

The relationship between a firm's operating profit/operating assets depends first of all on two other important relationships (ratios) namely that between its operating profit and its sales, and that between its sales and its operating assets.

Ratio 2 shows *what* profit margin has been earned on sales, whilst ratio 3 shows *how often* the margin has been earned on assets in the year. Ratio 3 shows how many times assets have been turned over in a year. Ratio 3a indicates the assets required per £1 000 of sales.

Thus the return on operating assets of a firm depends on the relationship between its ratios 2 and 3, this in turn depends on the relationships between its sales and its profits (and therefore its costs), and between its sales and assets, and therefore on the above ratios 2 to 9 and 3 to 18 respectively.

(2) *A Case of Progress*

Table A.2 shows the ratios of a light engineering firm for two years.

This looks like a success story: return on assets (ratio 1) has gone up from 8·2% to 9·8% due to a rise in both the firm's profit on sales (ratio 2) and its turnover of assets (ratio 3). The former has improved because the fall in the firm's production cost ratio 4 has been greater than the rise in

Table A.2

(Courtesy of the Centre for Interfirm Comparison Ltd. 1970)

	Year 1	Year 2
Return on assets		
1. Operating profit/Operating assets (%)	8·2	9·8
Profit margin on sales and turnover of assets		
2. Operating profit/Sales (%)	7·9	9·0
3. Sales/Operating assets (times per year)	1·04	1·09
Departmental costs (as a percentage of sales)		
4. Production cost of sales	78·3	77·1
5. Distribution and marketing costs	6·4	6·5
6. General and administrative costs	7·4	7·4
Production costs (as a percentage of sales value of production)		
7. Materials cost	33·8	33·7
8. Works labour cost	28·8	27·9
9. Other production costs	15·7	15·5
General asset utilisation (£'s per £1 000 of sales)		
3a. Operating assets	961	913
10. Current assets	524	479
11. Fixed assets	437	434
Current asset utilisation (£'s per £1 000 of sales)		
12. Materials stock	119	100
13. Work in progress	154	130
14. Finished stocks	35	40
15. Debtors	216	209
Fixed asset utilisation (£'s per £1 000 of sales)		
16. Land and buildings	201	200
17. Plant, machinery and works equipment	232	230
18. Vehicles	4	4

its marketing and distribution cost ratio 5. Ratio 4 has in turn improved as a result of falls in the firm's material, works labour cost and other production cost ratios (ratios 7, 8 and 9).

As to the firm's asset utilisation ratios there has been an improvement on both the current and fixed asset side (ratios 10 and 11). The rise in the finished stock ratio 14 is more than offset by falls in the materials stock, work in progress and debtors ratios 12, 13 and 15. Furthermore, the two major fixed asset investment ratios 14 and 17 have improved.

(3) *Shattered Illusions*

But the firm's illusion of success was shattered when it compared its ratios with those of other light engineering firms of its kind. Table A.3 is an extract from the results—it gives the figures of only seven of the thirty-five participating firms. Our firm's figures are shown under letter F; the seven firms on the table are similar in respect of size and products made; further-more, firm F and the other firms offer a wide range of products which are based on the assembly of several parts and components.

The firms whose ratios are shown in Table A.3 have used the same defini-tions of accounting terms and the same valuation principles, so that their ratios are comparable. They will for instance all have expressed the values of their plant and machinery in terms of current replacement values, not in terms of historical cost. This is important because the figures which appear in balance sheets do not necessarily indicate the true relative value of the fixed assets employed as between one company and another, and can therefore not be taken for interfirm comparison purposes. Depreciated book values cannot be used because they do not take into account the effects of inflation, and because depreciation policies and practices will differ between companies. Income tax written down values are not suitable because they are also based on original cost, and cost allowances have varied from year to year.

In addition to contributing the accounting data needed for the calcula-tion of the ratios, each of the seven firms will have provided background information about its policies and practices in such fields as production, marketing and distribution, about its size, product range, production processes and so on. This information makes it possible to understand the pattern of ratios of each firm, and to interpret differences between the ratios of firms.

As the IFC table shows, this year the firm's profit on assets is well below that of five other firms and this is due to both its profit on sales (ratio 2) and turnover of assets (ratio 3) being relatively low.

(4) *Interpretation and Guidance towards Improvement*

Like any firm taking part in this kind of IFC firm F has—with the com-parative table—received a confidential individual report explaining reasons for differences between the ratios of the seven firms, and drawing the attention of its management to possibilities for improvement. Among the points covered by the report were the following:

'You have stated that whilst in your year 1 sales of stock produced standard products represented 15% of your total sales, you had estimated that with more intensive marketing of these lines their sales might represent 20% of total sales in year 2. You expected that this would make it necessary to spend more on selling, but that the additional selling expenditure would be offset by production economies achieved through longer production runs. These longer runs would reduce idle hours (due to changes in machine set up) and thereby result in lower works labour costs, less work in progress and better machine utilisation. Furthermore, greater concentration on certain stock items would enable you to purchase some materials in larger quantities and therefore at lower prices. In fact, you found at the end of

Table A.3

(Courtesy of the Centre for Interfirm Comparison Ltd. 1970)

Ratios		A	B	C	D	E	F	G
Return on assets								
1. Operating profit/Operating assets (%)		22·9	20·7	16·6	13·1	10·3	9·8	4·2
Profit margin on sales and turnover of assets								
2. Operating profit/Sales (%)		18·9	18·0	14·4	12·4	9·9	9·0	4·7
3. Sales/Operating assets (times per year)		1·21	1·15	1·15	1·06	1·04	1·09	0·89
Departmental costs (as a percentage of sales)								
4. Production cost of sales		66·0	67·5	71·0	74·0	76·2	77·1	81·7
5. Distribution and marketing costs		8·2	7·9	7·4	5·9	6·0	6·5	5·6
6. General and administrative costs		6·9	6·6	7·2	7·7	7·9	7·4	8·0
Production costs (as a percentage of sales value of production)								
7. Materials cost		33·1	32·7	32·9	33·7	33·9	33·7	35·8
8. Works labour cost		18·8	21·1	24·2	25·1	26·8	27·9	29·4
9. Other production costs		14·1	13·7	13·9	15·2	15·5	15·5	16·5
General asset utilisation (£'s per £1 000 of sales)								
3a. Operating assets		827	872	866	942	958	913	1127
10. Current assets		448	469	477	529	524	479	654
11. Fixed assets		379	403	389	413	424	434	473
Current asset utilisation (£'s per £1 000 of sales)								
12. Materials stock		80	95	105	97	107	100	110
13. Work in progress		71	76	87	105	147	130	205
14. Finished goods stock		87	85	77	108	58	40	115
15. Debtors		210	213	208	219	222	209	224
Fixed asset utilisation (£'s per £1 000 of sales)								
16. Land and buildings		188	207	190	197	200	200	214
17. Plant and machinery		185	191	194	213	221	230	256
18. Vehicles		6	5	5	3	3	4	3

Firms

the year that sales of these stock lines had not represented 20% but only 18% of your total sales.'

'These developments would seem to explain the rises in your finished stock ratio 14 and your distribution and marketing cost ratio 5 as well as the falls in your production cost ratios (ratios 4, 8 and 9), your materials stock (ratio 12), your work in progress (ratio 13) and your plant investment (ratio 17). Furthermore, you seem to have taken action to improve your debtors ratio (ratio 15).'

'As you will see from the comparative table, your stock investment ratio 14, though higher than last year, is the lowest of the seven firms; furthermore, your marketing cost ratio 5 is lower than those of the more successful firms (A to C). In fact, the apparently less favourable ratios of these firms reflect their policy of reducing production planning problems through production in economic runs for stock of both finished products and certain components which are common to a fairly large number of their end products—and making a greater marketing effort in order to sell these stock products. Whilst, as you have stated, your company also manufactures certain components for stock, the percentage of finished stock sales achieved by you (i.e. 18% of your total sales) is considerably lower than the corresponding percentages of firms A to C. Thus, whilst as the background information provided by you indicates, your sales of products which are neither made for stock nor can be assembled from standard components represent 67% of total sales, the corresponding percentages of firms A to C are 21, 33 and 41 respectively.'

'These figures largely explain why your works labour cost, other production costs, work in progress and plant investment ratios 8, 9, 13 and 17 compare unfavourably with those of firms A to C.'

'If you would work towards the policies of these firms you would be able to improve your capacity utilisation and could raise your level of sales with your existing production facilities. You will see from the pattern of ratios of firms A to C that the adverse impact on the primary ratio of higher finished stock investment and marketing ratios can be offset by the lower ratios related to production which could be achieved with the policy adopted by these firms.'

The report also suggested ratio targets towards which firm F could work in the short term by changing either its finished stock policy or its policy with regard to the standardisation of components or both.

The example shows how the management of a firm can benefit from participation in an interfirm comparison through which its attention is drawn to weaknesses in its policy and performances, and which gives it ratio targets likely to result in a higher return on operating assets.

The Report to participants in the Light Engineering IFC of the Centre would, of course, be much more detailed and extensive since it would take account of the additional ratios and background data referred to above. Here are some examples of the kind of data used in order to explain to participants why their ratios differ from those of others in their industry. Such explanations are given

(1) by presenting ratios in respect of component parts of major cost of

asset items, e.g. showing a breakdown of pyramid ratio 6 into such ratios as Warehousing costs/Sales; Transport costs/Sales; Promotional costs/Sales; Other selling costs/Sales.

(2) by providing other subsidiary data which are selected because they will reflect the impact of certain factors likely to affect the pyramid ratios. Examples of such data are listed below:
(a) Works labour cost per works employee (£)
(b) Sales value of production per works employee (£)
(c) Value added per works employee (£)
(d) Composition of labour force
(e) (i) make versus buy policy in respect of components
    (ii) analysis of materials costs by type of materials used
(f) Depreciation of plant and machinery
(g) Average number of days' consumption of raw materials in stock
(h) Average number of days' supply of finished products in stock
(i) Average period of credit granted (days)
(j) Value of land and buildings per square foot (£)
(k) Sales per square foot
(l) Utilisation of plant and machinery
(m) Average age of plant and machinery
(n) Degree of mechanisation
(o) The proportion of export to total sales
(p) Sales/Production policy, e.g.
    (i) predominantly offering a small range of standard products made in economic runs in anticipation of orders
    (ii) predominantly offering a wide range of products and making for stock in anticipation of orders those items in the range which could be assumed to be in continuing demand
    (iii) predominantly offering a wide range of products and making for stock in economic runs the standard components common to different end products
    (iv) not offering a range of product, but manufacturing products as wanted by the customer.

Furthermore, differences between the ratios of firms are also interpreted by reference to such general factors as size and method of marketing.

It is of course possible to conduct interfirm comparisons relating to specific areas of a firm's activity (e.g. comparisons of labour productivity, of costs per unit of output or per operative and of relative efficiency in transport or distribution). Each of these sectional comparisons can be integrated into a general management comparison of pyramid ratios or can be made the subject of a self-contained scheme.

A.3 Questions Arising

(1) Confidentiality

How do IFC data become available? Clearly their availability depends first of all on the willingness of firms in an industry to contribute their figures to an outsider, the organisation conducting the IFC; but are firms not afraid that this will do them harm? There are several answers to this question.

First of all, several thousand firms in more than eighty industries in this country have already contributed their figures for IFC purposes to the Centre and other organisations conducting IFC apparently without suffering any harm, because the following steps are taken to ensure the anonymity and the confidentiality of their data participating firms contribute their figures anonymously, i.e. under code numbers given to them by the organisation conducting the IFC. This organisation uses the figures of firms to calculate ratios or percentages which are then shown, under code numbers, on tables like that of Table A.2. Such presentation in the form of ratios reduces the possibility of identification. That ratios do not disclose the actual figures of firms taking part in an IFC is shown by the following consideration: a firm's sales may have been £100 000 with a capital of £50 000; another firm's sales may have been £20 000 with a capital of £10 000; in both cases the ratio of sales to capital will be 2:1 (or a capital turnover of two times per year).

Furthermore, the ratios shown in IFC tables are unlikely to be the same as those which might be calculated from published accounts, because most of the information on which the IFC ratios are based is not given in published accounts, and because, for the purposes of the comparison, such key items as the figures of profit and assets (both fixed and current) are defined in a special way. Also, in the interests of confidentiality the IFC ratios are made available to participating companies only.

(2) *Accounting Comparability*

This leads to the next question already touched on in the previous paragraph: Are the figures of participating firms comparable? Will not the fact that firms may use different bases for, e.g. the valuation and depreciation of assets, the definitions of 'sales' and items of cost, destroy the comparability of their figures?

The answer to this question is that in a properly conducted IFC all participants will calculate their figures on the same uniform bases prepared for them and in consultation with them by the organisation conducting the exercise; the figures contributed by individual firms are carefully checked and any query arising is fully discussed with the firm concerned.

(3) *Similarity of Firms*

Even if successful arrangements can be made regarding the accounting comparability of firms taking part in an IFC, will the firms themselves not be different in respect of, for example, their size, stock policy, degree of mechanisation, marketing methods? Would the fact that there are such differences between these firms rule out IFC? There are people who say: 'Like should be compared with like, no two firms are really alike and therefore IFC's are useless'. Is this true? Are IFC's ruled out unless the firms are all of the same size, make the same products in the same way, operate in the same locality, employ the same kind of plant, use the same methods of distribution, etc.?

The answer is that the object of IFC is not to compare firms as such but to reveal what effect certain differences in their features and practices have on their performance. In fact, if there were no differences between the firms taking part they could learn nothing from the comparison.

Some major dissimilarities between firms (e.g. size) can be dealt with by means of grouping, i.e. by tabulating together the ratios of firms which have a major characteristic in common, but there are practical limits to such grouping if more than one or two dissimilarities have to be taken into account. These are best treated by way of individual interpretation of ratio differences on the basis of background information which is obtained from participants. Individual interpretation is an essential ingredient of a successful IFC and many of the organisations conducting IFC in this country would not confine their activities to the issue of comparative tables as such. The confidential reports given to each participating firm and certain other follow-up activities are integral parts of an interfirm comparison for management.

E

Orders and Minimum List Headings

(Extract from *Standard Industrial Classifications*, Revised Edition 1968, H.M.S.O.)

Minimum
List
Heading

Order I—Agriculture, Forestry, Fishing
001   Agriculture and horticulture
002   Forestry
003   Fishing

Order II—Mining and Quarrying
101   Coal Mining
102   Stone and slate quarrying and mining
103   Chalk, clay, sand and gravel extractions
104   Petroleum and natural gas
109   Other mining and quarrying

Order III—Food, Drink and Tobacco
211   Grain milling
212   Bread and flour confectionery
213   Biscuits
214   Bacon curing, meat and fish products
215   Milk and milk products
216   Sugar
217   Cocoa, chocolate and sugar confectionery
218   Fruit and vegetable products
219   Animal and poultry foods
221   Vegetable and animal oils and fats
229   Food industries not elsewhere specified
231   Brewing and malting
232   Soft drinks
239   Other drink industries
240   Tobacco

*Minimum
List
Heading*

Order IV—Coal and Petroleum Products
261   Coke ovens and manufactured fuel
262   Mineral oil refining
263   Lubricating oil and greases

Order V—Chemicals and Allied Industries
271   General Chemicals
272   Pharmaceutical chemicals and preparations
273   Toilet preparations
274   Paint
275   Soap and detergents
276   Synthetic resins and plastics materials and synthetic rubber
277   Dyestuffs and pigments
278   Fertilizers
279   Other Chemical industries

Order VI—Metal Manufacture
311   Iron and steel (general)
312   Steel tubes
313   Iron castings, etc.
321   Aluminium and aluminium alloys
322   Copper, brass and other copper alloys
323   Other base metals

Order VII—Mechanical Engineering
331   Agricultural machinery (except tractors)
332   Metal-working machine tools
333   Pumps, valves and compressors
334   Industrial engines
335   Textile machinery and accessories
336   Construction and earth moving equipment
337   Mechanical handling equipment
338   Office machinery
339   Other machinery
341   Industrial (including process) plant and steelwork
342   Ordnance and small arms
349   Other mechanical engineering not elsewhere specified

Order VIII—Instrument Engineering
351   Photographic and document copying equipment
352   Watches and clocks
353   Surgical instruments and appliances
354   Scientific and industrial instruments and systems

Order IX—Electrical Engineering
361   Electrical machinery

58

Minimum
List
Heading

432	Leather goods
433	Fur

Order XV—Clothing and Footwear
441	Weatherproof outerwear
442	Men's and boy's tailored outerwear
443	Women's and girl's tailored outerwear
444	Overall's and men's shirts, underwear, etc.
445	Dresses, lingerie, infants' wear, etc.
446	Hats, caps and millinery
449	Dress industries not elsewhere specified
450	Footwear

Order XVI—Bricks, Pottery, Glass, Cement, etc
461	Bricks, fireclay and refractory goods
462	Pottery
463	Glass
464	Cement
469	Abrasives and building materials, etc, not elsewhere specified

Order XVII—Timber, Furniture, etc
471	Timber
472	Furniture and upholstery
473	Bedding, etc
474	Shop and office fittings
475	Wooden containers and baskets
479	Miscellaneous wood and cork manufactures

Order XVIII—Paper, Printing and Publishing
481	Paper and board
482	Packaging products and paper, board and associated materials
483	Manufactured stationery
484	Manufactures of paper and board not elsewhere specified
485	Printing, publishing of newspapers
486	Printing, publishing of periodicals
489	Other printing, publishing, bookbinding, engraving, etc

Order XIX—Other Manufacturing Industries
491	Rubber
492	Linoleum, plastics floor-covering, leathercloth, etc
493	Brushes and brooms
494	Toys, games, children's carriages, and sports equipment
495	Miscellaneous stationers' goods
496	Plastics products not elsewhere specified
499	Miscellaneous manufacturing industries

60

Minimum
List
Heading

879   Other professional and scientific services

Order XXVI—Miscellaneous Services
881   Cinemas, theatres, radio, etc
882   Sport and other recreations
883   Betting and gambling
884   Hotels and other residential establishments
885   Restaurants, cafes, snack bars
886   Public houses
887   Clubs
888   Catering contractors
889   Hairdressing and manicure
891   Private domestic service
892   Laundries
893   Dry cleaning, job dyeing, carpet beating, etc
894   Motor repairers, distributors, garages and filling stations
895   Repair of boots and shoes
899   Other services

Order XXVII—Public Administration and Defence
901   National government service
906   Local government service

PART 2   A COMPARATIVE PRODUCTIVITY
ANALYSIS OF LABOUR AND MACHINES

Chapter 6

Manufacturing Industry Productivity Levels

Net output per employee is a productivity measure used by the
Board of Trade economists in their Census of Production statistics,
and it was the publication,[53] in January 1966, of certain extracts
from the 1958 Census which gave the tentative conclusion that
regional variations in the net output per person employed were
large enough to warrant a cause study. This prompted the former
Department of Economic Affairs to sponsor a comparative productivity analysis of manufacturing industries in the West Midlands.

The 1958 statistics summarised in Table 6.1 showed the net
output (or added value) per employee for the West Midlands to be
lower than the national average in ten of fourteen groups of manufacturing industries listed. Only four regions—Scotland, the North
West, Yorkshire and Humberside and the East Midlands were
ranked lower. A more recent analysis—Table 6.2—of the 1963
Census of Production Statistics published in August 1970 indicates
that the West Midlands' position has worsened with only two
regions, Yorkshire and Humberside and the East Midlands ranked
lower.

The ten manufacturing groups include metalworking, engineering
and electrical industries—industries that are highly concentrated
in the West Midlands and employ over 70% of the total manufacturing working population. The same industries play a major role
in the supply of materials, sub-assemblies and finished products
to other regions and to export.

There has been an increased rate of growth in the value of net
output per employee between 1958 and 1963 shown in Table 6.1
and 6.2. For Great Britain this amounted to £354. The Chemical
Industry was the largest contributor (£732), with Food (£416)

Table 6.1 INDEX NUMBERS OF THE VALUE OF NET OUTPUT PER PERSON EMPLOYED FOR EACH INDUSTRY GROUP AND REGION 1958

S.I.C. Order		North	North West	Yorks and Humberside	West Midlands	East Midlands	East Anglia	South East	South West	Scotland	Wales	Great Britain	Great Britain Net Output per Employee
III	Food, drink and tobacco	84	100	83	98	109	83	106	115	104	82	100	1263
IV	Chemical and Allied	113	106	91	81	77	82	104	79	93	85	100	1656
V	Metal Manufacturing	102	91	98	90	100	61	101	72	93	128	100	1213
VI	Engineering and Elect.	104	102	100	95	99	100	100	95	103	100	100	1006
VII	Shipbuilding	113	108	101	97	161	111	95	87	94	96	100	825
VIII	Vehicles	65	85	95	107	90	129	108	93	87	84	100	1047
IX	Metal goods n.e.s.	94	99	94	92	111	137	115	89	102	95	100	931
X	Textiles	105	86	109	113	106	92	119	133	94	210	100	723
XI	Leather goods, furs, etc.	97	96	94	75	120	77	105	113	101	110	100	796
XII	Clothing and Footwear	90	88	87	100	108	100	117	97	87	88	100	583
XIII	Bricks, Pottery, Glass, Cement, etc.	94	114	110	74	102	106	118	80	100	100	100	975
XIV	Timber and Furniture	92	92	88	95	89	94	113	88	88	75	100	835
XV	Paper, printing and publications	89	94	90	87	81	89	111	93	88	94	100	1065
XVI	Other manufacturing industries	85	103	82	102	106	67	96	142	93	102	100	918
	Total manufacturing industries	108	95	94	97	92	97	108	100	96	118	100	
	Total manufacturing industries net output per employee	1095	963	954	979	936	984	1089	1010	973	1193		1009

Table 6.2 INDEX NUMBERS OF THE VALUE OF NET OUTPUT PER PERSON EMPLOYED FOR EACH INDUSTRY GROUP AND REGION 1963

	S.I.C. Order	North	North West	Yorks. and Humberside	West Midlands	East Midlands	East Anglia	South East	South West	Scotland	Wales	Great Britain	Great Britain Net Output per Employee	Increase 1958—1963 £	%
III	Food, drink and tobacco	84	100	86	96	108	98	100	107	112	92	100	1679	416	32
IV	Chemical and Allied	112	107	82	77	75	111	105	83	99	82	100	2388	732	44
V	Metal Manufacturing	91	92	95	97	105	92	100	88	96	119	100	1449	236	19
VI	Engineering and Elect.	92	93	95	96	107	84	105	98	99	113	100	1307	301	30
VII	Shipbuilding	98	111	96	164	125	87	106	100	91	95	100	1060	235	28
VIII	Vehicles	69	89	82	101	69	110	117	119	96	85	100	1455	408	38
IX	Metal goods n.e.s.	92	94	97	95	107	119	111	101	97	96	100	1218	287	31
X	Textiles	175	83	104	117	97	103	115	157	91	201	100	1060	337	46
XI	Leather goods and fur	90	92	108	70	110	90	106	123	90	102	100	1105	309	38
XII	Clothing and footwear	100	92	88	94	106	92	111	121	90	90	100	771	188	32
XIII	Bricks, pottery, glass, cement, etc.	98	111	103	76	105	108	110	89	99	100	100	1354	379	38
XIV	Timber, furniture	94	94	92	93	94	95	110	87	90	86	100	1138	303	36
XV	Paper, printing and publication	85	94	84	83	82	93	112	87	86	107	100	1449	384	36
XVI	Other manufacturing industries	94	100	87	109	90	85	97	119	98	99	100	1301	383	41
	Total manufacturing industries	104	96	91	95	91	99	109	101	97	113	100			
	Total manufacturing industries net output per employee														
	£ Increase	1425	1311	1244	1304	1238	1338	1495	1388	1331	1540		1363	354	
	% 1958—1963	330	348	290	325	302	354	406	378	368	347				35
		30	36	30	33	32	36	37	37	36	29				

and Vehicles (£408). It is not difficult to recognise that these industries have a comparatively high capital/labour ratio but only the chemical industry tends to operate twenty-four hour shift-working. At the other end of the Table, metal manufacturing (£236), shipbuilding (£235) and clothing and footwear (£188) show a slow growth in net output per employee. It should be remembered that the cost of living over this same period rose by 15%.

With regard to regional improvements, the South East and South West (between 1948 and 1958), continue to show faster growth in both employment and net output, obviously influenced by the industrial development in new towns and London overspill areas. Scotland also has a higher than average growth and is similarly influenced by the industrial development policies of the past Government. In the Yorkshire and Humberside region the growth attributable to net output per person employed is disappointingly slow and well below the national average (£290 as compared to £354). The West and East Midlands are also similarly placed with a lower than national average growth of £325 and £308 respectively.

Are these statistics evidence of a serious regression in our major industrial areas and is the index being used as the economists intended?

As a measure of productivity net output per employee is inadequate and can be quite misleading in industrial and regional comparisons. Industry in general is becoming more capital intensive and output per head is more dependent on how well the plant and equipment are utilised. Little headway has been made in measuring capital utilisation or productivity, or even to the measurement of labour and capital in a combined sense. It is because of this deficiency that comparisons can be inconsistent and unreliable.

Our search for productivity levels began by investigating whether the total number of employees, and consequently the index, might be influenced by the numbers that worked part time. The evidence collected showed that such labour had an insignificant effect but studies in other industries (e.g. clothing and footwear) may prove the opposite. Therefore in order to accommodate this probability future employee calculations should be adjusted for part time working and preferably calculated in financial terms.

Capital factors were found to greatly influence the productivity of various industries in the different regions. For example, Table 6.2 shows the net output per employee index for textiles in Wales as 210% that of the national average. The most notable reason for this very high performance is the capital intensity in the nylon spinning plants. The same is true for metal manufacture which is shown as 128% that of the national average. Both groups consequently influence the region's productivity index of 118% for the total manufacturing industries.

Part of the differences arising from capital intensities may be removed by converting the number of employees in terms of man hours into financial units and to add to this capital depreciation, ensuring that the depreciation is derived on the basis of current replacement values and not historical cost. That is:

$$\frac{\text{Net output (or added value) per annum}}{\text{Total wages, salaries and benefits} + \text{Capital depreciation}}$$

In disagreement with the Industrial Policy Group[54], the major influences appear to be the industry structure and product processes employed which we found to act in different ways in different industries. In the West Midlands there tends to be a higher than average horizontal integration, which is a situation in which various processes are divided among a number of specialist firms. In the engineering industry the first stages of production tend to be highly competitive[55] and their prices strictly controlled by the larger consortia, which are often the larger vehicle assembly plants. This can cause a low net output in the early stages of manufacture at the expense of the final stages. There appears to be a predominance of the early stage engineering production in the West Midlands (in contrast to other regions), which supplies industry throughout the country.

What is true of the engineering industry appears to be true of the iron and steel industry which is also a major contributor to the region's total output. In this industry the lower than average net output per employee (90% in 1958 and 97% in 1963), is due to the type of product traditionally produced. The cause is partly the large number of firms, many of them private, which carry out re-rolling and finishing processes with little support of crude steel production. Where there is a concentration of firms dealing with lengthy finishing processes the net output per employee will be lower than those regions producing crude steel. For example the ratio of finished steel produced to crude steel produced was 1·433 in the West Midlands compared to 0·740 for the U.K.

Although we found only 41% of the machines productively utilised in adding value to throughput materials (our standard of comparison being two shift operation in engineering and electrical manufacturing and three shift operation in the metalworking industries), there were some differences between the industries. For example iron and steel (42%), non ferrous (46%), electrical (30%) and engineering components (45%). There was even a wider range between individual firms within a given industry, than between the industries. The highest utilisation in any firm being 66% and the lowest 17%.

In terms of potential productive utilisations (taking the best individual firm's average as potential) it is considered that net output (or added value) per employee could be increased by over 60% (if there was no compensating increase in the number of employees). Thus for the West Midlands sample this would mean a percentage increase of 61%.

The utilisations of labour were: productive (48%); attending (11·5%); handling (19·5%); other work (5·0%); idle—waiting management (5·5%) and idle—operatives responsible (10·5%). The productive labour utilisation differences between firms in an industry (23% to 71%) were more significant than the differences between industries: iron and steel (43%); non ferrous (45%); electrical (50%) and engineering components (55%). If the best firm's labour utilisation was taken as the potential then the net output (or added value) per employee could well be increased by nearly 48%. This however would require some introduction of low cost automation and better organisation of work. Thus for the West Midlands sample this would mean a percentage increase of 47·8%.

Chapter 7

Study Background

The collection of facts in British industry, manufacturing in particular, is a hazardous task. Anonymity must be ensured, firms coded and statistics disguised. There are fears that competitors may break the codes and learn information that could be detrimental to the company. There are also fears that Government may have access to information which will enable them to know more than would be required under the normal company law and taxation statutes.

This attitude was found to be strongly in evidence in the West Midlands especially when attempts were made to obtain basic accounting measures, such as 'Total Sales' values and 'Total Expenditures' external to the company.

The research project was introduced to the manufacturing companies of the region at a time when the industrial situation was causing some concern. Following a troubled Winter which saw two major take-overs, widespread redundancies and sporadic strikes, the Spring of 1968 was viewed with some pessimism. The economic situation was at its lowest ebb for many years. The Prices and Incomes Policy was causing a great deal of discontent and the administration of increased taxation (S.E.T.) and training levies seemed overwhelming to some small and medium sized companies. Productivity bargaining with its associated changes in the structure of earnings; changes from piecework and/or timework to measured daywork and standard time systems were rapidly affecting the traditions of shop floor activity. Unemployment was at its seasonal height.

In the vehicle component group (S.I.C. 381) strong trade union reaction was met, particularly in companies involved in the Leyland/B.M.C. merger. Rumours of redundancies were at that time quite strong and 30 000 jobs were considered in jeopardy by the national press.

The views expressed by Turner[56] are relevant. He suggests that the major contribution to labour unrest in car firms has been the acts and omissions of individual companies. He cites the early post-war agreements of Standard and Ford Motors, which although commendable at the time, helped in later years to form the background to labour disputes. There is also criticism of some plant managers who respond to sectional disputes by laying-off more uninvolved workers than is necessary—an action that is in evidence today. Instability and inequality of earnings, and irregularity of employment are also important factors contributing towards labour unrest.

So, it was inevitable that in meetings with the executives of more than a hundred firms, more than half immediately refused to co-operate on the grounds that it was inconvenient at that time. Frequent comments were: 'not interested'; 'undergoing reorganisation'; 'negotiating productivity agreements'; 'investigations already in hand by the Prices and Incomes Board (Motor Vehicle Group), management consultants and other universities and colleges'.

One company director expressed the views of others when he complained bitterly of continually receiving requests and circulars from Government Departments, Consultants and other organisations. His staff were far too busy with Government paperwork to collect more information. He thought (without consideration of the objectives of the project), that his company would not benefit in any way.

Furthermore where executives had thought it unnecessary to have worker representatives present at meetings, and had relied upon the excellence of their labour relations, it was found in most cases that the investigators had to repeat the talks with shop stewards and stewards committees. Indeed there were occasions when explanations had to be given to groups assembled in canteens and elsewhere, needless to say without great success. Arguments for rejection at this point were exclusively related to 'it might have been different if we had been brought in at the beginning'.

In conclusion the opinion was formed that many executives did not wish to disturb what were already regarded as unsteady labour relations. Several managers and foremen objected to the studies because they were too involved in their own inadequate systems of decision and control. Foremen in many companies were seen to carry out their own production planning and control services, and their attempts to schedule or match loads against machine capacities relied heavily on judgement guided by past experience.[57] The allocation of production resources was frequently left to the foremen whose job description more befitted a working chargehand since they often set up the machines and delivered the materials. Very rarely was there a document system or visual aid to determine utilisation of labour and machines, or to progress the product and spotlight delays. It was not uncommon that sales departments had a strong influence in determining the production plan and product progress. Frequent demands for changes of plan and no defined forecasting system were evident. Without a well defined planning and control function a firm has to rely upon local and intuitive solutions rather than on factual information and feedback control. Production batch sizes were often governed by customer's order, or by fixed quantities loaded at regular intervals, and it was not uncommon to see that batch allocation was generally made on 'one operation per batch per week cycle'. No doubt the operatives welcomed this simply because frequent re-setting for new work would prejudice their weekly earnings, especially where bonus schemes were in operation.

Trade Union and other employee representatives objected to the studies specifically pointing to 'Government influence in universities', and believing that the results would be used against them, either by management in a labour productivity purge or Government in their economic policies for regional development.

Nevertheless, a final count showed that twenty-four company directors and their personnel, some with curiosity and reservations agreed to co-operate despite the fact that each foreman in each company would be required to participate for a continuous period of four weeks.

It was pointed out in discussions with the foremen that it was additional work but the knowledge gained in this relatively new technique would enable them to know more of what went on in their section, and they would be able to control 'down-time' more objectively. The difficulties encountered in a foreman's working day were appreciated, but it was emphasised that for the project to be a success it was necessary to rely on their full co-operation.

F

Chapter 8

Sample Mix

The twenty-four participating firms ranged in size from 200 to 3 000 employees; some were labour intensive, some capital intensive and others a mixture. Table 8.1 shows the distribution of firm size within the study. The observations were carried out during the month of May 1968, which was considered to be a representative period between the Easter and Whitsun statutory holidays—a period that has since been shown by the Central Statistics Office as representative in the light of an upward trend in output per head.

One or two studies were inevitably delayed because of the extensive discussions on co-operation and also to organise a period convenient to the company. The four week period of sampling was chosen partly for the foremen who were reluctant to sample for a longer period.

Some firms were more co-operative than others and the generosity of a few who allowed more departments within their firms to be studied (thereby involving more foremen and more samples), resulted in the project gaining more stature. Table 8.2 shows the distribution of departments by type and industry.

The activity sampling technique was introduced to the foremen during a discussion period supplemented by a visit to each department in order to illustrate the method of 'snap-shot' reading, and to clarify the finer points of factor definition. This was necessary because it was known that each production method had its own peculiarities, and individuals had their own definition for productive and non productive work. For example, 'handling' to some foremen was recognised as 'operating' and was considered to be adding value to the product. These views had to be corrected and acceptable interpretations of activities clearly impressed.

During the visit to each department a selection was made of direct operatives from a prepared list. Some men and women

Table 8.1 DISTRIBUTION OF SIZE OF FIRM BY NUMBER OF EMPLOYEES

No. of Employees	Metalworking Iron and Steel V	Metalworking Non-Ferrous V	Electrical Machinery and misc. VI	Engineering Motor Vehicle (Components) VIII	No. of Firms
S.I.C. m.l.h.	311	322	361 and 367	381	
200— 299		2	1	1	4
300— 399	1	1	2		4
400— 499	1	2			4
500— 999	1		2	1	4
1000—1499	1	1		1	4
1500—1999			1	2	2
2000—2999		1			1
3000—3999	1				1
No. of Employees	7 447	5 631	4 296	4 122	21 496
Total No. of Employees in West Midlands (1963)	26 500	51 600	75 000	150 100	303 200
Percentage Involved in Studies	2·8	10·9	5·7	2·7	7·0

Table 8.2 DISTRIBUTION OF DEPARTMENT TYPES WITHIN SELECTED INDUSTRIES—LABOUR AND MACHINES

Department type	Iron and Steel V—311		Non-Ferrous V—322		Electrical VI—361/369		Motor Vehicle VIII—381		Total		
	*L	M	L	M	L	M	L	M	L	M	Combined
1 Machine Shops		1	4	5	5	9	9	9	18	24	42
2 Press Shops (Heavy)	2	2	2	2		1	1	1	5	6	11
3 Press Shops (Light)			2	2	5	8			7	10	17
4 Assembly Shop (Heavy)	3				3		4	3	10	3	13
5 Assembly Shops (Light)	3		2	1	14	6			19	7	26
6 Rolling Mills	2	16	7	6					9	22	31
7 Extrusion Presses			6	7					6	7	13
8 Dressing and Finishing			3	3			1		4	3	7
9 Painting		1			3		1	1	4	3	7
10 Furnaces and Heat Treatment		3	5	7		1			5	10	15
11 Drawbench and Reeling			11	9					11	9	20
12 Miscellaneous Services (Stores, Maintenance, Inspection, etc.)	1		4	1	1		1		7	1	8
13 Wire Mills and Wire Drawing			1	3					1	3	4
Totals	11	23	47	46	31	25	17	14	106	108	214
Totals Combined	34		93		56		31		214		
No. of Firms	6		7		6		5		24		
Average No. of Departments per Firm	5·6		13·3		9·3		6·2		9·0		

(* L denotes labour and M machines)

were in mixed groups, but where there was an opportunity to compare utilisations between men and women and these were treated as separate groups as for example in electrical assembly work. The machines were selected at random while walking around the department. It was considered that the selection made by the researchers would be random, whereas if it had been the foremen the choice might well have been biased towards a selection of productive machines, knowing that they would be continually operational for the period of sampling.

Chapter 9

Activity Sampling

'The technique of activity sampling provides a simple and effective way to measure productive and non productive time . . . and to permit the measurement of labour and facilities utilisation'.[36]

Under conventional application activity sampling implies two factors—working p and not working $1 - p$. Calculations are normally performed to determine the number of observations n required to ensure that the findings of the chosen factors are within close confidence limits of accuracy. For most industrial measurements a confidence level of 95% is considered satisfactory, which means: 'one is confident for 95% of the time that the random observations n will represent the facts, and for 5% of the time they will not'.[58]

It is important to realise that observations need not always be made at random. Tippett[59] says: 'very often the pattern of behaviour of the system is so irregular that randomisation of the observations is unnecessary. . . . Randomisation is achieved only at a cost: the cost of handling the hundreds (or thousands) of random numbers, and the cost of the observer making himself available at random instants'. For example the operations within a manually controlled process are not necessarily regular, constant and/or repetitive. Observations under these conditions might very well be made at regular intervals, providing such regularity does not pick up cyclic patterns. What is already random cannot be made more random. Only in machine controlled processes where regular cyclic patterns are more likely to occur does it become important to use random number tables.

Other practical suggestions have been made for determining sample size; 'rule 1 000' described by Rowe[60] is known to give satisfactory results in industry as long as there is no desire to measure accurately small percentage activity occurrences.

It was on the basis of these arguments that it was decided to ignore the conventional approach of activity sampling. It was considered impractical for 140 foremen in 24 establishments to observe and record at predetermined times having random intervals, and still satisfactorily meet their duties of supervision. This was especially as instructions were given that the indicators (numbered discs) identifying which activity should be observed, were to be drawn at random within a specified hour at the foreman's convenience spread over the hour. It was emphasised that observations should not be concentrated into one small part of each hour.

9.1 'DISC-O-TEC' SAMPLING

DISC-O-TEC activity sampling was the first of its kind attempted on such a large scale in Britain. The use of foremen to carry out observations in addition to their normal duties was considered novel. Foremen were being requested to do something in an ordered fashion, which they themselves do in their normal duties; that is, observe men and/or machines working. The following is an extract from instructions issued to foremen who agreed to participate in the exercise.

For this exercise we will supply each participating foreman with:

(1) sample study sheets for each hour of his working shift, or working day whichever method is decided upon in discussion.
(2) a maximum of twenty discs, each to represent an operative, machine or work station.

During *each hour* the foreman will withdraw a handful of discs from a pocket (about 4 or 5) at random intervals of his own choice, select a disc number, identify it with man or machine and take a mental snap-shot of the activity marking the study sheet accordingly. The foreman must continue to do this until all discs have been transferred from one pocket to the other in one hour. This must be repeated for all subsequent hours in his working shift, for a period of four normal working weeks.

In order to simplify the analysis of data, the study sheets (appendix C) were designed as data processing cards and arranged to incorporate six major activities embracing productive and non-productive work:

Facility (or Machine) Sheet Heading:
    (1) Forming, removing material and/or   Machine
        joining or separating material   Productive

(2) Setting or inspecting—job change new product

(3) Tool adjustment—no job change

(4) Maintenance—planned and unplanned
    Waiting for maintenance, and
    Maintenance in progress

(5) Machine Idle—operative not responsible
    Set-up and
    Non set-up

(6) Machine Idle—operative responsible

} Machine
  Non Productive

Men (or Labour) Sheet Headings:

(1) Operating—man in control of process   Man Productive

(2) Attending

(3) Handling

(4) Servicing—cleaning down, changing tools, doing own inspection, etc.

(5) Waiting at work station—management responsible
    For work
    For service
    Idle—no work

(6) Waiting at, or away from work station— worker responsible

} Man
  Non Productive

Each activity is described in Appendix C.

It was considered that as the discs were transferred from one pocket to another, ordered stacking might occur and the last disc to be looked at in one hour's sampling could be the first selected in the hour following. Shuffling was suggested, but finally tests were carried out using two groups of subjects, 20 in each group. One group sampled with shuffling and the other without. In each case the order in which the discs were sampled was noted. A statistical analysis proved that ordered stacking was insignificant.

An illustration of how recordings were made on the study sheets is shown below. In order to show comparisons of utilisations, hour by hour, day by day and shift by shift the method of recording was divided two ways:

(1) by shift hour and time

(2) by day

Shift hour and time were related to mornings, days, afternoons and nights as shown in Table 9.1 and in order to overcome the differences in starting times of each firm, the shift hour (1 to 8) was adopted as the basis for comparison. Comparisons on a day basis presented no problems.

Once the shift hour and time had been recorded on the study sheet, the same sheet was used for the *same hour every day* for the

Table 9.1 SHIFT HOUR AND TIME RELATIONSHIP

Shift	Time	Shift Hour
Mornings	06.00 to 07.00 h	1
	07.00 to 08.00 h	2
	13.00 to 14.00 h	8
Days	08.00 to 09.00 h	1
	09.00 to 10.00 h	2
	16.00 to 17.00 h	8
Afternoons	14.00 to 15.00 h	1
	15.00 to 16.00 h	2
	21.00 to 22.00 h	8
Nights	22.00 to 23.00 h	1
	23.00 to 24.00 h	2
	24.00 to 01.00 h	3
	05.00 to 06.00 h	8

period of sampling. Separate sheets were used for each remaining hour. This meant that each observer chosen to sample in this way was issued with 8 sheets 'man' type and/or 8 sheets 'facility' type.

To obtain day trends, the observers were issued with 5 sheets 'man' type and/or 5 sheets 'facility' type. Monday was nominated day 1 and so on. Once the day had been recorded on the study sheet, the same sheet was used *every hour during the nominated day*, i.e. if the sheet was recorded day 1 then it was used every hour each Monday for the period of sampling. Separate sheets were used for day 2 and so on. Saturday, Sunday and overtime working were omitted from the study. Tea breaks (morning and afternoon) where these were taken, and the time immediately before and after each break,

Table 9.2

'men' type study sheet

Identifi- cation	Disc No.	Operating			Handling		Waiting		Away	
Joe	11	ЖЖ ЖЖ ЖЖ		ЖЖ	1		111			24
John.	12	ЖЖ 111		1111		ЖЖ 111	1111			24
Janet	13	ЖЖ 1111		ЖЖ	11	ЖЖ	111			24
Total		32		17		16		7		72
Utilisation %		44·4		23·6		22·2		9·8		100

'facilities' type study sheet

Identifi- cation	Disc No.	Operating		Tool Adjustment		Breakdown	No Work		
Drill	1	ЖЖ 1		111		1	ЖЖ ЖЖ 1111		24
Lathe	2	ЖЖ ЖЖ ЖЖ 1	ЖЖ	1		11			24
Press	3	ЖЖ ЖЖ ЖЖ 1111	111			1	1		24
Total		41		12		4	15		72
Utilisation %		57		17		5·5	20·5		100

including lunch and end of shift, were also ignored. An example of how recordings were made is shown in Table 9.2.

In all 24 firms the 140 foremen approached their task willingly, taking a total of 273 116 observations over a period of four weeks. Many remarked that after a few days they found the knack and could visualise how useful the technique could be. Some inevitably found it laborious and were pleased to see the end of sampling, but at the same time thought the experience had been worthwhile. The majority viewed the sampling method as an effective means of finding out more about their own department and would have liked more time with longer intervals between observations to apply it.

Chapter 10

Analysis and Results

The sales values, external purchases, and total number of operatives and staff were obtained from each of the twenty-four participating firms. From these figures the average net output (or added value) per employee indices were determined for each industrial group and for the West Midlands sample, Table 10.1.
The results of the utilisations of labour and machines are illustrated in Figures 10.1 and 10.2. They show the comparative trends of productive activity by hour and day respectively. The Pie-Charts illustrate the proportions of the available time occupied by the six activities.
Figure 10.2 exhibits a saddle-back profile which is usually

Table 10.1 NET OUTPUT PER EMPLOYEE—COMPARISONS FOR INDUSTRY AND WEST MIDLANDS SAMPLE

S.I.C.	*m.l.h.*	*Industry*	*United Kingdom*		*West Midlands*		
			1958 £	1963 £	1958 £	1963 £	1968 £
VI	311	Iron and Steel	1347	1507	1182	1580	2146
	322	Non Ferrous	1090	1491	1091	1222	2058
IX	361	Electrical Machinery	1042	1102	994	1085	⎫
	369	Electrical Miscellaneous	922	1239	832	1126	⎬ 1787
XI	381	Motor Vehicle (components)	1204	1692	1172	1563	2106
		West Midlands (sample) Average					2022

associated with the typical productive output curve. The saddle-back being characteristic of manual controlled work within a specified working period, starting at a low level, increasing to a steady plateau and then falling at the end of the work period.

Dudley[34] explains: 'the shape of the saddle-back output curve is to be accounted for largely, in lost time due to ancillary work, operational delays, and to a lesser extent on personal delays'.

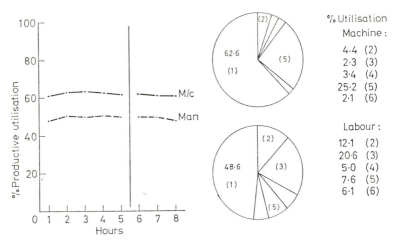

Figure 10.1 *Summary of West Midlands firms labour and machine utilisation by the hour* (*S.I.C.* 311, 322, 361, *and* 369, 381)

The saddle-back profile is shown to occur between the first and fifth hours of the working shift. The remaining three hours—sixth, seventh and eighth—indicate a constant and regular decline, suggesting that less productive work is done towards the end of the shift. Only in the iron and steel industry was there evidence of a rise between the seventh and eighth hours. One reason for this might have been the influence of furnace temperature and billet soaking time on the production control of rolling mill processes.

Where multiple activities (embracing occasional as well as those of a repetitive nature) are observed simultaneously in a fixed 'economic' period of sampling, it is inevitable that reasonable limits of confidence in the results are only possible for the more frequently occurring activities. Limits of confidence tend to be waived for the least frequent in the interests of economy of sampling time.

Inspection of Tables 10.2 and 10.3 show that where it has been possible to obtain reasonable limits at a 95% confidence level, these are indicated in the results.[58] The number of observations recorded appears in parentheses.

Adjustments

It has already been pointed out that activities during tea breaks (morning and afternoon), and the time immediately before and after such breaks, including: beginning-of-shift, lunch-time and end-of-shift, were not observed. Thus it was considered reasonable

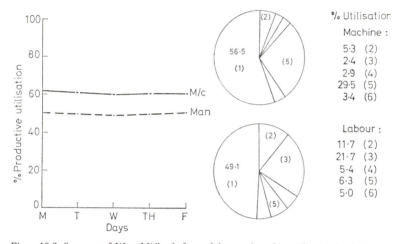

Figure 10.2 Summary of West Midlands firms: labour and machine utilisation by the day

to adjust the labour 'Waiting—operative responsible' and the machine 'Idle—operative responsible' activities, by an additional 5% each. It is generally accepted by management that an allowance be given for tea-breaks and for changing, getting to work station at the beginning-of-shift, leaving work station and changing at end-of-shift. For instance:

10 minutes morning coffee
10 minutes afternoon tea
2 minutes beginning-of-shift
2 minutes end-of-shift

Total 24 minutes in a 480 minute day—equivalent to 5%.

Table 10.2 UTILISATION OF LABOUR

| Industry | Activity | | | | | | Total No. of Observations made |
	Operating 1	Attending 2	Handling 3	Servicing 4	Waiting—Management Responsible 5	Waiting—Operative Responsible 6	
Iron and Steel	51·3±3·5 (3 694)	9·7 (713)	18·5 (1 915)	3·8 (364)	10·5 (843)	6·2 (456)	(7 985)
Non Ferrous	47·5±1·5 (23 824)	17·7 (8 478)	16·5 (9 860)	5·7 (2 754)	9·0 (3 200)	3·6 (2 451)	(50 567)
Motor Vehicle Components	61·0±1·5 (12 534)	9·4 (2 291)	13·6 (3 628)	4·2 (1 062)	3·8 (962)	8·0 (1 479)	(21 956)
Electrical	60·4±1·0 (15 616)	7·1 (1 803)	16·3 (7 027)	3·2 (1 443)	4·9 (1 524)	8·1 (2 241)	(29 654)
West Midland Sample	49·1±0·5 (55 668)	11·7±0·5 (13 285)	21·7±2·5 (22 430)	5·4±12·5 (5 623)	6·3±9·0 (6 529)	5·0±11·0 (6 627)	(110 162)

Table 10.3 UTILISATION OF MACHINES

| Industry | Activity | | | | | | Total No. of Observations made |
	Productive 1	Setting 2	Tool Adjustment 3	Maintenance 4	Idle—Management Responsible 5	Idle—Operative Responsible 6	
Iron and Steel	63·1±0·5 (46 027)	9·9 (8 617)	4·4 (3 659)	3·9 (3 378)	12·3±7·5 (7 900)	6·4 (5 828)	(75 409)
Non Ferrous	64·2±0·5 (31 076)	3·3 (1 276)	2·2 (899)	5·7 (2 101)	23·4±3·5 (12 327)	1·2 (761)	(48 440)
Motor Vehicle Components	72·2±0·5 (10 149)	3·7 (576)	2·3 (546)	2·0 (371)	17·3±9·0 (2 349)	2·5 (482)	(14 518)
Electrical	54·5±2·0 (12 969)	6·0 (1 489)	1·8 (653)	2·1 (395)	33·3±3·0 (8 489)	2·3 (392)	(24 587)
West Midlands Sample	62·2±0·2 (100 221)	4·4 (11 958)	2·3 (5 757)	3·4 (6 245)	25·2±2·0 (31 110)	2·1 (7 663)	(162 954)

Furthermore, machine productive utilisation could be improved by revised shift working arrangements. It is reported in a survey[61] that: 'Shiftworking enables management to obtain much higher production and consequently a higher rate of return on capital invested'. However, important social and organisational factors have yet to be considered.

It was found that shiftworking policies were highly significant (99%) in the utilisation of machines. A three shift working policy was mostly in evidence in the metalworking industries, and a two shift working policy in both the vehicle and electrical manufacturing industries. To provide a fair comparison of utilisations between industries, the data of the Iron and Steel and Non Ferrous firms could be adjusted where necessary to a constant three shift working policy, and the data of the vehicle and electrical firms adjusted to a constant two shift working policy.

The adjusted results are shown in Tables 10.4 and 10.5 (page 86).

Summary of Tabular Information

Inspection of Table 10.4 shows that there is a relatively high level of ancillary work in each industry—work which does not contribute to the 'added value' activities in the manufacture of the products. For example, the 'handling' and 'attending' activities of the West Midlands labour sample, together account for over 30% of the total time available—equivalent to more than 62% of the actual utilised productive activity (48%). In addition to this, 'Waiting—management responsible' accounts for 5.5% of the total time.

Inspection of Table 10.5 and the West Midlands sample shows that 45% of machinery is idle, or spare, at any point in time reinforcing the view that management are unaware of the financial implications arising from inadequate planning and controls, which consequently influence all forms of management decision making. The Electrical group—the industry with the lowest net output (or added value) per employee—indicates large idle, or spare, machine capacity (59%) and it appears that this industry could provide the greatest contribution to productivity by applying modern management techniques. This evidence supplements the report[27] that the ratio of sales to fixed capital assets was found to be much lower in British electrical and electronic firms than that of comparable American firms.

Maintenance and tool adjustment time in the sample absorb 4%, while setting (or job changeover—indicating the variety in job orders and batch quantities) accounts for 4.5%. Together this

Table 10.4 ADJUSTED UTILISATION OF LABOUR

Industry	Activity						Productive Individual Firm %	
	Operating %	Attending %	Handling %	Servicing %	Waiting—Management Responsible %	Waiting—Operative Responsible %	Lowest	Highest
Iron and Steel	43·0	8·0	24·0	4·5	10·5	10·0	23·0	66·0
Non Ferrous	45·0	16·0	18·5	5·0	6·0	9·5	29·0	71·0
Motor Vehicle Components	55·0	10·0	15·5	4·5	4·5	10·5	42·0	60·0
Electrical	50·0	6·0	23·0	4·5	5·0	11·5	36·0	71·0
West Midlands Sample	48·0	11·5	19·5	5·0	5·5	10·5	23·0	71·0

Table 10.5 ADJUSTED UTILISATION OF MACHINES

Industry	Activity						Productive Individual Firm %	
	Productive %	Setting %	Tool Adjustment %	Maintenance %	Idle—Management Responsible %	Idle—Operative Responsible %	Lowest	Highest
Iron and Steel	42·0	7·5	3·5	3·5	36·0	7·5	28·0	62·0
Non Ferrous	45·0	2·5	1·0	3·0	44·0	3·5	17·0	66·0
Motor Vehicle Components	45·0	3·0	2·5	1·5	41·0	7·0	32·0	65·0
Electrical	30·0	4·0	1·5	1·0	59·0	4·5	24·0	42·0
West Midlands Sample	41·0	4·5	2·0	2·0	45·0	5·5	17·0	66·0

time is equivalent to over 20% of the time the machines are productively applied.

Potential Increase in Net Output per Employee

If the percentage utilisations of non productive activities were reduced to the lowest recorded by any one company within each industrial group, then the average productive utilisation of labour and machines might well be improved as in Table 10.6 (page 88).

These figures also compare to an average increase in Net Output (or added value) per Employee (Table 10.7).

Table 10.7

Industry Group	Current (1968) Added Value £	Potential Added Value £ Labour	Machines	Increase % Labour	Machines
Iron and Steel	2146	3249	3168	53	48
Non Ferrous	2058	3247	3018	57	47
Motor Vehicle Components	2106	2718	3042	30	44
Electrical	1787	2144	2207	20	40
West Midlands Sample	2022	2991	3255	48	*60

* Based on the productive utilisation achieved by the best company in the region

Comparative Utilisation by Department Types

Thirteen department types were chosen to represent the variety of production processes found to exist in our sample. Inevitably some were studied more often than others as shown in Table 10.8 (page 89).

Machine shops and rolling mills were the most frequently observed departments, the most infrequent (one only) being miscellaneous services. This of course was to be expected, for miscellaneous includes such work as maintenance, inspection, stores and warehouse activities which are all highly labour intensive. It is an area that requires further research to find ways of making the services more capitalised.

Inspection of Table 10.8 suggests that highly capitalised equip-

G

Table 10.6

	Iron and Steel		Non Ferrous		Motor Vehicle Components		Electrical		West Midlands Sample	
	Current %	Potential %	C %	P %	C %	P %	C %	P %	C %	P %
Labour	43·0	66·0	45·0	71·0	55·0	71·0	50·0	60·0	48·0	71·0
Machines	42·0	62·0	45·0	66·0	45·0	65·0	30·0	42·0	41·0	66·0

Table 10.9 OPERATIVES/STAFF RATIO COMPARISONS

S.I.C.	m.l.h.	United Kingdom						West Midlands Average of Sampled Firms		
		1958			1963			1968		
		Operatives No.	Staff No.	Ratio	Operatives No.	Staff No.	Ratio	Operatives No.	Staff No.	Ratio
V	311	227 400	48 200	4·7:1	216 100	56 300	3·8:1	5 590	1 860	3·0:1
	321 322	98 000	29 800	3·3:1	101 300	31 000	3·0:1	3 690	1 940	1·9:1
VI	361 369	218 300	89 000	2·4:1	238 000	103 600	2·2:1	3 030	1 270	2·4:1
VIII	381	275 000	65 300	4·2:1	329 100	90 300	3·6:1	2 820	1 290	2·2:1
Average for Selected Group				3·5:1			3·2:1			2·4:1

Table 10.8 COMPARISON BY DEPARTMENT TYPE OF PERCENTAGE PRODUCTIVE UTILISATIONS

Industry / Dept. Type	No. of Depts. sampled	Iron and Steel %	Non Ferrous %	Vehicle Components %	Elect. %	Highest Ind. Dept. %	Lowest Ind. Dept. %	Average %	Rank
Department Type Machine Utilisations									
M/c Shops	24	43	31	57	33	69	17	35	10
Heavy Press	6	31	84	36	26	84	26	55	6
Light Press	10		44		27	44	23	37	8
Heavy Assy.	3			31		31	31	31	11
Light Assy.	7				28	35	19	28	12
Rolling Mills	22	37	68			61	28	57	5
Extrusion Press	7		39			66	27	39	7
Dress and Finish	3		66			66	66	66	1
Paint	3	42		34		42	34	38	8
Heat Treatment	10	62	54			65	40	59	4
Draw and Reel	9		60			67	46	60	3
Miscellaneous	1		27			27	27	27	13
Wire Mill	3		65			65	65	65	2
Department Type Labour Utilisations									
M/c Shops	18		41	47	44	59	34	44	8
Heavy Press	5	50	40	63		63	40	50	6
Light Press	7	65	50		47	51	42	49	7
Heavy Assy.	10	31	71	67	60	76	49	63	1
Light Assy.	19	23	34		65	74	12	60	2
Rolling Mills	9		37			40	13	30	13
Extrusion Press	6		38			62	13	37	11
Dress and Finish	4		26	50		51	38	43	10
Paint	4		36	73		74	26	44	9
Heat Treatment	5				36	47	17	36	12
Draw and Reel	11	62	53			67	46	53	5
Misc. Services	7		42	66	55	66	20	53	4
Wire Mill and Draw	1		55			55	55	55	3

ment such as rolling mills and extrusion presses are not as productively employed as one would expect. No evidence is available in manufacturing industries to support the general claim that highly capitalised equipment is more productively employed than lower valued equipment.

The department types were ranked in order of best utilised and from the machine samples it can be seen that the most productive are within the metalworking groups—dressing and finishing, wire and tube drawing, reeling, heavy presswork and rolling mills, indicating a wide range of capital values. What is most surprising is that machine shops—predominant in engineering—appear in the lower categories of utilisation in both labour and machine samples.

Comparative Utilisations of Male and Female Operatives

The possibility of equal pay for women is now regarded as a reality. But not all working women feel that equal pay will solve the inequality which consigns them to jobs of inferior skill. To them it is not so much pay, as an opportunity to be accepted in skilled jobs of a superior value and at the same time to dispel the Victorian impression that women are physically incapable of doing the same work as men. Young[62] considers that the implementation of equal pay for women may mean that women cannot now be regarded as slave labour undercutting men's rates for the same job. It holds a promise that employers may be compelled to do what many have never done for themselves: use their female labour efficiently.

It was observed during the investigation that large numbers of female operatives were employed in the industries studied. Relatively few however, were seen to be doing jobs alongside men. The majority were employed on light assembly activities, light presswork, inspection viewing and packaging—jobs that are frequently recognised as being more suitable for women and at the lower end of the pay scale.

In the electrical industry an opportunity was made to compare the utilisation of direct female operatives with those of direct male operatives working on light assembly activities. Six studies were conveniently arranged in selected firms to enable these comparisons to be made and where workbench layouts, motions employed and environment were almost identical. Ignoring the rate, or intensity of performance, females were found to be more productive when at their work stations (57%) than male operatives (49%), but at the same time took twice the amount of rest pauses away from their stations (females 9% and males 4%). However, before employers think to replace male assemblers with females and female close rest rooms (which were observed to be exceptionally well furnished in comparison to male rest rooms) further research on the rate of performance needs to be carried out.

Operative/Staff Ratio Comparisons

There is a conscious effort by a few companies to keep the Operative/ Staff ratio under reasonable control. One such company controls its number of staff to less than 10% of the total employees, while a similar one, which is both technologically competent and progressive, is not aware of the importance of this control.

Inspection of Table 10.9 shows this ratio to be on the decline. Whether the trend is the result of increased mechanisation, influence of 'Parkinson', administration of increased taxation and training levies needs further investigation.

Chapter 11

Factors Affecting the Rate of Output

It is recognised that the degree and intensity of labour and machine utilisation is an important contribution to the rate of output. Some firms operate at performance levels higher than others, which may well require more sophisticated planning of costs, especially those resulting from a more rapid machine depreciation leading to increased maintenance and expensive replacement policies. There is also increased expenditure on consumable tools, more handling equipment, etc. Such high performance levels must be economically justified by properly designed and meaningful costing systems.

A survey of machine tool utilisation by Tinker[63] shows that 42% of capstan lathes studied had a turning capacity of over 6 inches diameter, yet only 2% of the entire work he checked needed a machine of this size. In another report[64] he shows that in equipping a workshop little attention is paid to the size of workpiece. 'The machine tools are in general not particularly well chosen for the work they have to do. Much more use could be made of smaller and simpler machine tools with consequent savings in such items as capital cost, heat, light, power, rent, rates, and maintenance and replacement costs. Indeed, it would seem possible that the total cost of machining could be cut by 20% to 30% if the machine tools used were properly matched to the work they have to do'. Another significant fact from the same report was that: '... over all the machines surveyed, the time spent in setting and handling was approximately two-thirds of that spent cutting, and this could seem to be the most significant area for improvement of efficiency'.

In some recent research carried out by the Productivity Research Unit of Birmingham University on power presses, similar results were found where work carried out on a 25 ton press group in a plant employing 54 presses, only 14% had a tonnage requirement of over 15 tons. A summary of the findings is given in Table 11.1.

In general large capacity machine tools, in addition to incurring more capital expenditure and occupying more space, have higher operating costs than smaller machines. This cost is based on the assumption that the real value added to throughput materials by productive equipment is the value that would have been added by using the optimum size machine for that class of work.

Furthermore, we found that machine tools were not operating under the most economic machining conditions. A study undertaken in the engineering components industry, analyses economic machining conditions of a sample of machine tools and compares them with a 'Hi-E' range which combines a number of factors to

Table 11.1

Press Group (tons)	Range (tons)	Press Capacity Utilised %
25	15·1 to 25	14
15	10·1 to 15	24
10	6·1 to 10	34
6	3·1 to 6	28

provide a selection of cutting speeds and feeds to obtain the lowest cost per piece machined, best tool life and minimum 'floor-to-floor' time. In working within the 'Hi-E' range, while it is desirable to operate at surface speeds in excess of 400 ft/min, only 8% of capstan and turret lathes, 16% of automatic lathes and 20% of copying lathes were run in the optimum range.

Stephenson[65] is reported as saying that on average, valuable machine tools stand idle for 80% of the time. Some companies have been seen to spend as much as £50 000 on a machine to do a job that could be done just as well on one costing little more than half this sum. He also considers that plant layouts and planning and control systems (where these are employed) are often out-dated and inadequate for modern manufacturing requirements.

Other research currently being carried out by Swan[66] into manufacturing businesses of the Yorkshire and Humberside region, suggests that more than 50% of business failures are in fact due to a lack of knowledge of management techniques and information systems. His analysis so far suggests that where small companies (25/499 employees) employ method study and work measurement techniques together or combined with standard costing and budgetary control and/or value engineering, there is a significant positive correlation with success measured as a return on capital employed and/or growth in capital. His findings also suggest that of the fashionable production management techniques, such as variety control, inventory control, economics of machining, group technology and classification systems, something like 50% of production executives do not even know of them. Yet one could suggest that if the objective of most companies is to improve their return on capital or total earnings, then such techniques are necessary as a stepping stone for growth. Feather[67] claims: 'the progress made by unions in understanding management and production techniques and equipping themselves to deal with them, is very much greater than on the other side of the industry . . . Trade Unions are giving a lot of attention to equipping their representatives to deal properly with the current situation of increasingly rapid changes in both the technology and organisation of industry'.

Obviously, more education and training in the specific field of production management is essential, especially in the use of such techniques and the effective implementation procedures that go with them.

Frost-Smith and Marten,[68] and Stephenson[65] advance the view that there is more machine idle-time in companies who lack computerised scheduling facilities. However, there is no evidence in the Birmingham research so far, to support this view. Where computer scheduling has been found to be operational (and to agree with Frost-Smith they are relatively few) it tends to be inadequately employed. It would appear that there is a general lack of time measurement, particularly those measurements concerned with manual elements of work that programmers can call upon. Foremen in many companies carry out their own scheduling and loading of machines and therefore, until a well-defined function of production planning and control is in operation, with work measurement favourably accepted and objectively applied, computer scheduling will continue to be inadequate.

Before Productivity Bargaining

Profitable areas for improvement in efficiency as listed below should be considered by all managements before entering the area of productivity bargaining:

(1) *Improved Costing Systems.* Many companies, through inadequate costing systems are unaware of the real contribution which various

products and processes make to the overall company objectives. Furthermore, in many of the companies studied, there was little or no effective cost control. Most of the firms in the sample which had recognisable cost systems use a labour/overhead absorption method which pays little or no attention to the influence of capital intensive facilities on product costs.

The Chairman of Jessel Securities, in an interview with Welham[69] talks of one company as typical of many today which 'was run for 50 years by one chap who had no idea what anything cost to manufacture. We only had to put in the most elementary costing techniques and make improvements in the overall running of the business . . . Profits went up from £136 000 to £500 000 in a single year'.

(2) *Rationalisation of Product Variety.* In one large iron and steel company producing 1 500 varieties of steel specification (and this did not include individual sizes and dimensions), less than 10% of the 1 500 items were all that were needed to meet the technical requirements of their customers. We also found in the electrical firms, predictably enough, that less than 20% of the products contributed over 80% of the added value. Not only does rationalisation improve efficiency, it can reduce inventory and set-up costs as well as improving quality standards.

(3) *Improved Production Scheduling and Control, and Inventory Control.* Research carried out by our unit with the assistance of postgraduates found that foremen in many companies carry out their own production planning and control function. Their attempts to schedule or match loads against machine capacities rely heavily on judgement guided by past experience. The methods of forecasting were rule-of-thumb, and it was not uncommon to see that sales departments had a strong influence in determining the production plan and progress of products, Large quantities of work-in-progress were often seen to be occupying space that could be more productively applied, thus indicating a lack of inventory and variety control. The control of such work could reduce working capital requirements and consequently improve the rate of turnover which is the sales/working capital ratio.

(4) *Low cost Automation, Improved Mechanical Handling and Pre-tooling Arrangements.* On the evidence that 'handling' and 'attending' activities amount to over 30% of the operative's working day, there is a strong case for low cost automation equipment, which could

reduce this time and thus release more man hours for productive work.

(5) *Economics of Machining and Group Technology.* Comparing machining conditions with a 'Hi-E' machining range and thereby operating the capital to some optimum condition, can give large potential gains as can introducing a classification system ready for the installation of a computer, with production scheduling and family grouping of components, thus encouraging flow-line methods of plant layout and manufacture. Reducing set-up times, increasing batch sizes, reducing work in progress and handling time, administrative costs and so on.

(6) *Value Engineering and Analysis and Improved Materials Utilisation.* In the electrical group we found that an evaluation of the materials used in switchgear, fractional horse-power motors and accessories, gave yields of the principal materials which ranged from 50% to 92% in steel; 42% to 79% in copper; 55% to 64% in brass and 68% to 75% in plastics. Through scrap and waste reduction, improved utilisation and purchases, value engineering can help firms reduce substantially the total amount of materials and expenditure.

(7) *Improved Maintenance Systems and Replacement Policies.* Installation of a complete planned maintenance system may not be necessary. But corrective and preventive maintenance to machinery was found to be critical in the flow-process of a product, and this is an area which needs to be considered. Standardisation of parts moreover, helps to reduce capital tied up in spares. Method study of repairing activities reduces delay time.

Before recourse to the complications of productivity bargaining more accurate methods of assessing productivity to emphasise the extent of potential gains need to be made. Relevant measures are necessary to pin point areas of inadequacy and to show how much progress can be achieved. Experience in the West Midlands shows that significant benefits are there to be realised, not just in this region, but in the whole of U.K. industry.

The Completion of Study Sheets

Firm: write in the name of the firm in which you are employed.

Department or Section: some departments are complete in themselves and in charge of one Foreman, e.g. machine department, maintenance department, or assembly department. If this Foreman is carrying out the study in the whole of the department then simply write in *the name of the department.* If, however, the department consists of two or more sections, each having its own Foreman, then in this case, write in *the name of the department and the section,* e.g. machine department, press section.

For the purpose of our studies the Departments or Sections may be:

(1) labour intensive—male and female working in assembly or on maintenance work.

(2) capital intensive—automated facilities.

(3) labour and capital combined—machine shops, offices, etc.

For case (1) the Foreman will be required to sample labour and will therefore be issued with 'men' type study sheets only. For case (2) the Foreman will be required to sample machines and will be issued with 'facilities' study sheets only. For case (3), the most frequent occurring case, the Foreman will, therefore, be issued with both types of study sheet.

The maximum number of items to be studied in any case (1), (2) or (3) will be 20, even though the department or section may have more than 100 men or facilities.

The selection of items for study will be carried out by the researchers ensuring that the selection is representative, i.e. a cross-section of his department or section. It is suggested that lists be prepared of 'facilities' and of 'men' and the selection made at random, say every third or fifth machine or man on the list.

Observer: every observer who uses the sheet must write in his grade and name, even when the observer changes shifts.

Definitions of Activities listed on the Study Sheet

First, identify each disc number with 'man' or 'facility', selected as representative of the department or section. Write alongside each number, listed in the left-hand column of the study sheet, the name, type, or code of item to be observed. At the instance of observation the Foreman must accurately decide under which factor, listed on the study sheet, the activity taking place most closely resembles. *It is important to record the mental 'snap-shot—what you see at the instance of observations—not what you think will immediately follow or what has gone immediately before.*

Forming, removing material, and Joining: refers to press forming, metal cutting machines and assembly or welding machines; all of which might be operated under the following conditions:

    (1) *Without Operator*—an automatic machine.

    (2) *Operator Active*—turning handwheels, pushing buttons, pulling or pushing levers.

    (3) *Operator Inactive but Present*—standing-by to control when the occasion arises.

Setting or Inspecting

    (1) *Job Change—New Product:* refers to the machine being set-up for a new job, or where a 'first-off' is being produced or inspected. (Includes stripping down).

    (2) *Adjustment—No Job Change:* refers to an instance when tools are being adjusted or changed without changing the job. Or, inspecting immediately after adjustment.

Maintenance—Planned and Unplanned: the Foreman receives an instruction when a facility is to have Planned Maintenance carried out, and will therefore know, at the instance of observation, whether the facility is undergoing Planned or Unplanned Maintenance.

    (1) *Waiting Maintenance:* repairs may or may not have started but at the instance of observation no maintenance is being done and therefore the facility must be waiting maintenance.

    (2) *Maintenance in Progress:* on other occasions of observation repairs may be being carried out.

Machine idle—Operator not responsible

    (1) *Set-up:* a facility may have previously been set-up, but at the instance of observation could be in a stopped condition, because:

        (a) an operative has not been assigned to the job

        (b) an operative has been assigned, but sent away for materials, tools, or other job needs, on the instructions of the Chargehand, Foreman or Management

        (c) waiting other services, such as inspection, handling, etc.

    (2) *Not Set-up:* if the machine is not set-up at the time of observation

there must be no work for it and is therefore considered to be purely *idle*—operator not responsible.

Machine idle—Operator responsible: a facility with a job in progress and an operative assigned to it, could be in a stopped condition as the result of the operative taking rest, wasting time or away from his station.
  At the instance of observation an operative might be at his work station, i.e. bench, machine, or conveyor station, etc.

Operating: refers to joining parts together, pushing or pulling levers, turning handwheels, or pushing buttons, i.e. adding value to the product and controlling the process.

Attending: refers to a machine minder, although the operative manually controls a machine most of the day, at the instance of observation he may be standing-by just watching ready to take over control when the occasion arises.

Handling: refers to making ready material, loading or feeding material to a machine, reaching out picking up parts and positioning ready for assembly or machining.

Servicing: refers to the occasions when the operative might be reading instructions from a drawing, or specification, or job card, receiving instructions from the Chargehand, Foreman, or Manager. Carrying out his own inspection or marking-out, in fact doing work that other skills are employed to do.

Waiting Work: where the Chargehand or Foreman has assigned the operative to a job and at the instance of observation is seen to be waiting for the job at the machine or bench.

Waiting Service: where the operative is observed to be waiting at his machine or bench for inspection, setter, or maintenance, etc. Also, at the instance of observation the operative may be conspicuous by his absence away from his work station, bench, or machine; where:

Worker Responsible: at his own decision, i.e. personal needs, rest, etc.

Worker Not Responsible: where the operative has been requested, by the Chargehand or Foreman, to collect materials, tools, drawings, specification, or other job needs, or requested to do other work away from his regular work station.

Idle—No Work: only the Foreman or Chargehand knows when an operative has not been assigned to a job, even though the operative appears to be busy on some 'foreigner' or homework at the instance of observation, and therefore the operative must be considered idle—no work.

FIRM:							DEPARTMENT OR SECTION :							OBSERVER :		
SHIFT HOUR : TIME : DAY :		AT WORK STATION				WAITING AT STATION		AWAY FROM WORK STATION		IDLE NO WORK	OTHER REMARKS					
MEN		OPERATING	ATTENDING	HANDLING	SERVICING	WAITING FOR WORK	WAITING FOR SERVICE	WORKER RESPONSIBLE	WORKER NOT RESPONSIBLE							
	1															
	2															
	3															
	4															
	5															
	6															
	7															
	8															
	9															
	10															
	11															
	12															
	13															
	14															
	15															
	16															
	17															
	18															
	19															
	20															
TOTALS																

FIRM:
SHIFT HOUR:
TIME:
DAY:

DEPARTMENT OR SECTION:

OBSERVER:

FACILITIES	FORMING, REMOVING MATERIAL AND JOINING			SETTING OR INSPECTING		PLANNED MAINTENANCE		UN-PLANNED MAINTENANCE		MACHINE IDLE			OTHER REMARKS
	WITHOUT OPERATOR	OPERATOR ACTIVE	OPERATOR INACTIVE PRESENT	JOB CHANGE NEW PRODUCT	ADJUSTMENT NO JOB CHANGE	WAITING FOR MAINTENANCE	MAINTENANCE IN PROGRESS	WAITING FOR MAINTENANCE	MAINTENANCE IN PROGRESS	OPERATOR NOT RESPONSIBLE SET-UP	OPERATOR NOT RESPONSIBLE NOT SET-UP	OPERATOR RESPONSIBLE	
1													
2													
3													
4													
5													
6													
7													
8													
9													
10													
11													
12													
13													
14													
15													
16													
17													
18													
19													
20													
TOTALS:													

PART 3   PRODUCTIVITY BARGAINING AND
INCENTIVES

Chapter 12

Economics of Incentives

Arising from their research the authors are of the opinion that
the area for improvement in productivity is large enough—without
increasing capital investment—to warrant a serious examination
of the objectives of management and employees. It would generally
follow that management should organise all the available resources
towards an improvement, while employees should give their fullest
co-operation. Unfortunately, it cannot be shown that the employee
will identify his interests with those of management without the
discipline of close control and/or the inducement of an incentive.

  There exists a rooted conviction among managers that money is
the only significant means of motivating employees. The International Labour Office[70] points out: 'there is evidence from a
number of industries and countries that payment by results is often
associated with relatively high productivity'. However it may be
that both these are a function of a third factor—good management.
Davidson, Florence, Gray and Ross[71] point to a similar conclusion.
The Polish economist Pohorille[72] writes that in any society (capitalist
or socialist), 'the best way to raise labour productivity is through
a wage system in which wages depend directly on work and its
results'. Contradictory to this, the Soviet authority, Kapustin[73]
suggests that in modern industry there is a very appreciable shift
from piecework to time work', and Brown[74] describes some of the
advantages that could be gained from this. Experiments are under
way in Cuba and China using moral incentives but it is difficult
to gauge the success or the relevance of such schemes.

H

In Israel, to overcome the disincentive of high taxation on earnings from incentive schemes, an income tax law was passed whereby lower rates of taxation were charged for wages earned under approved payment schemes and work norms. The Israel Institute of Productivity played an active role in implementing the law which provided a great stimulus to productivity.

McGregor,[75] Likert[76] and Revans[77],[78] all point to the influence of good human relations as a means of improving employee morale and productivity. However, as Vroom and Deci[79] point out: 'there is the continuous problem that at any given point in time people vary in the extent to which they are willing to direct their energies towards the attainment of organisational objectives'.

Incentive schemes aim at bringing the objectives of individuals into accord with those of the organisation of which they are part. Ideally in maximising their own objectives they should also maximise the objectives of their company. The importance of relating objectives to successful managerial performance is advocated by Humble[80] in his system of 'Management by Objectives'.

12.1 SYSTEM OBJECTIVES

Industrial-commercial systems exist to achieve some definite purpose. One of the criteria for determining the objectives of any such system would be that, which when not satisfied, prevented the system from functioning. Productive systems fail to function not when they fail to show a profit, but when they are unable to pay the salaries of their personnel. The provision of earnings for all the people who enable a productive economic system to function imposes a primary demand on the revenue generated by the system's conversion of basic materials M, into saleable products S. Generating the maximum total earnings $(T = S - M)$, which is the value added to throughput materials is one of the major objectives of such systems. It is from these earnings T, that all salaries L, and capital charges K, are provided and profits P, distributed.

The unitary concept of an industrial-commercial system uses the team analogy to describe a firm with all the members having only one focus of loyalty—their management as leaders. In return the leaders have a reciprocal obligation to their followers. This unitary view does not however describe the actual situation in industry. Even if it did, there would be a duty to staff and worker that would transcend the simple profit objective.

The pluralistic concept accepts that society (including business systems) is made up of sectional groups with divergent interests and supports the view that there are very few common objectives between the different group interests. 'Sectarian interests are inevitable in any highly specialised society' writes Ross,[81] but continues, 'the task of management is to reconcile various sectional interests as closely as possible to the central objective in order to enable the firm to work efficiently towards that end'. Boyd[82] writes: 'If workers are to be recognised as co-owners—not because they own shares but because they own their jobs—then the responsibility of management to workers can be no less than the responsibility to shareholders'. As both profits and remuneration are included in total earnings (engineers added value), or conversion output, there is a common interest among the various sections of industry in maximising these. However there may be conflicting interests in sharing these earnings.

Total earnings maximisation is compatible with the major economic objectives of most developing economies or societies:

(1) providing employment (wages and salaries)
(2) increasing per capita income
(3) increasing the gross national product
(4) increasing export earnings through adding value to indigenous materials by processing
(5) generating surplus earnings (or national profits) for investment in national development
(6) conserving foreign exchange through import substitution

Smith and Beeching[16] write that the objective of industry, 'is to provide the goods which the community requires at the lowest possible cost measured in terms of expenditure of real purpose'. Even if one accepts the view that the production of goods for the community at the lowest cost is industry's primary objective, it would be necessary to deduct the materials (and outside expenses) from the sales value of the goods in order to avoid calculating over and over the materials throughput costs. The net output is really the value added to throughput materials, which correspond to the total earnings objectives.

Even if as stated by Galbraith,[83] the objective of mature industrial management is to generate enough surplus revenue to ensure sufficient dividend and growth to satisfy the stockholders and thereby maintain autonomy, this surplus must come out of a net output which exceeds the conversion costs. Growth, net output and social earnings objectives are included in total earnings concepts.

12.2 SOCIAL PRODUCTIVITY

Maximising systems earnings objectives does not always result in maximising the objectives of the super system in which it is part. Least cost objectives may be in conflict with maximising systems earnings objectives (higher wages may mean higher unit costs and prices).

Price rise by companies often conflict with social objectives such as price stability (or even reduction). Taking these objectives into account we can deduct the additional revenue T_{add}, due to the price increase from the total earnings (since it conflicts with social objectives) and arrive at a social productivity index:

$$\frac{T - T_{add}}{C} = \frac{T_{soc}}{C} \tag{12.1}$$

Often, enterprises provide certain economic benefits to society for which they may not get a financial reward, and so these do not enter into its total earnings. Sometimes the objectives of government subsidies, or tax reliefs are intended to bring social objectives into line with those of the firm. In grants to firms in development areas the purpose is to avoid wasting the large expenditure that already exists in their infrastructure. Intangible benefits to society at large may be included in total earnings comparisons made for macro social objectives.

Individual profitability of industry might lead to ultra centralisation of all industry in the Midlands or the London area. To do this would involve heavy social overhead expenditure in transport, housing, hospitals, schools and other public institutions—to the net loss of society, since existing facilities would be neglected. Government assistance to firms in the development areas may be considered as earnings of these firms for the indirect social benefits or savings they generate.

In recommending that efficiency (or productivity) be measured from the viewpoint of social economies Ruist[84] states: 'when the Government for example, talk about efficiency of business, it is thinking of what one might call social efficiency, and the total production is judged from the point of view of its social usefulness. Different groups may however have different views as to how this usefulness should be assessed and consequently as to whether a change in production implies an increase in efficiency or not'. Borch[85] reports: 'that some factories in Eastern Europe seem to use weights which are supposed to represent the social usefulness of the various products. . . . The purpose of using such weights to calculate productivity, is to encourage factories to produce the goods which are considered essential by the central planning authority. This means that the conversion factors are used as a kind of artificial price'.

The social least cost or price objectives can be accomplished by secondary adjustments to the net output values to bring individual firms into accord with the whole macro economic structure. Government may influence enterprise through preferential taxes, levies, technical assistance, protection and subsidies the objective being to bring into accord the earnings and profit objectives of the individual firm and the entire community. In this way the intangible, but real economic benefits that a firm generates, are considered. A firm thus seeking its own suboptimum objectives will maximise the national earnings objectives and increase the community's social productivity.

Chapter 13

Attitudes and Job Satisfaction

Incentives may be examined from two points of view:

(1) the creation of motivation to improve work performance
(2) the introduction of bonus payments for work performance above a certain standard

It may be thought that these two viewpoints are complementary, that the provision of the second creates the first and that the rest is a matter of reorganisation. Although support is advanced for this view, many doubt the simplicity of the relationship and examples of one situation existing without the other are evident.

Viteles[86] states: 'It has become increasingly evident that the worker seeks more than financial reward from his job and that the extent to which other needs and wants are satisfied, has a strong bearing upon how well a wage system will work in a particular situation, and exercises a direct and frequently predominating influence upon employee performance and satisfaction at work, and upon employee morale'.

In considering the first viewpoint it will be noticed that the emphasis is on achieving better performance as a result of motivating the worker in that direction. It does not pre-judge but rather begs the question—what is the appropriate motivation?

Individuals look for those aspects of jobs which are related to their own values, some placing greater value on security and others on income or type of work. But while individuals vary in their sets of values, research evidence shows there is moderate consistency in the values of specific groups. Such values are subject to changes depending upon social, economic and other influences.

Both management and trade union officials in their efforts to forecast and educate the needs of employees have been unable to make valid predictions. Nevertheless, where trade unions have been in competition with management negotiating the points both feel the employee wants from his job, the trade union has been eminently more successful.

13.1 ATTITUDE ASSESSMENT

A simple and introductory way of developing answers to what is the appropriate motivation is to present a list of factors to defined groups of workers asking them to rank each factor in order of importance. Paired comparison can be usefully applied in reducing the element of indecision when two or more factors must be sorted into position. Immediately after completion, the same individual within the group can be asked to answer spontaneously what are his likes and dislikes. Analysis of these comments should reveal the order of importance of some of the factors listed and if the answers have been given freely should compare within certain limits.

For example, such a survey might be designed around the following factors:

achievement
recognition
job content
responsibility
prospects (advancement)
salary or wage
status
working conditions
job security
continuous employment
improved relations with higher grades
improved relations with lower grades
company policy
administration
industrial relations

Questions requiring spontaneous answers

(1) Whenever you talk about your job, would you say that your comments are mostly favourable or unfavourable?
(2) How long have you been employed here?
(3) What is your age?
(4) Have you ever thought of leaving?
    (a) What caused you to think of it?
    (b) What stopped you going?

(5) What particular things do you like about your job?

(6) What particular things do you dislike about your job?

A priority list might also help to determine the type of fringe benefits needed within a defined group, for example:

annual salary increment
financial incentive
profit sharing
company stock shares
productivity agreement
house loan
longer holidays   Incentives
company car
contributory pension
non contributory pension
educational fees
luncheon vouchers
travelling expenses
interest free loan
promotion prospects
tours abroad on behalf of the company
paid leave to attend courses
sickness benefit

In 1967, Norman and Snaith[87] had an opportunity to undertake a research survey of employee attitudes, amongst more than two hundred building maintenance workers in small and medium sized municipal and private enterprises. They had listened to views expressed by senior staff, that direct labour compared their wages unfavourably with wages paid in local factories, and that this prevented recruitment and retention of suitable skills. The results, however, did not support these views.

Labour stability for the previous two years had been 65%, slightly more than the average stability statistics of 60% supplied by the then Ministry of Labour for local factories.

A standard list of questions was designed to determine the attitude 'satisfiers' and 'dissatisfiers'. The answers were to be used as hypotheses for further research. Two opening statements were used to establish whether employee attitudes were predominantly directed towards money satisfactions or job satisfactions:

'Which one of the two statements is more true to your needs?'

(1) A great deal of satisfaction in people's lives comes from the jobs they do. No matter how much money you get, if the job

itself is not a satisfying experience you remain discontented.

(2) People work so that they can lead a satisfying life away from work. No matter what the work is, if the money is right you won't worry.

These statements were supported by questions requiring spontaneous answers to the likes and dislikes of their jobs, and applied to higher or lower paid groups in other related and unrelated work.

The most liked aspects of building maintenance work were:— the variety of work—interesting work—fault finding aspects of the job—good conditions—permanent and continuous employment. The employee's statements gave no indication that they viewed other jobs with higher or lower wages as being related to themselves. A complete lack of interest was evident, whilst sympathy and some general discussion regarding more lowly paid individuals was evinced. Money was not (in the majority) specifically mentioned, although it was not a well paid job by local standards.

A vacancy in one of the companies had recently been refused by six external applicants, all of craftsman level and comparable to the men employed. This could imply that wages in this situation were at a level which compared unfavourably with the expectations of outsiders, and a small change in the internal or external situation could make the wage level a point of argument for this group.

Although only a survey, such a study reinforces the views expressed some years ago by Herzberg[88] and since extended by many workers, that money is not in itself a motivator, other than at a level where it is low enough to be an obvious source of dissatisfaction. Equally, if satisfaction from work is inadequate, then very often wages become important as a symptom of the situation of dissatisfaction, perhaps in an attempt to achieve compensation outside the work situation.

The variety of work was the most important factor in the jobs of the men interviewed. It is stated by students of job design that improved performance is achieved where men have responsibility for the outcome for their work sequence. A change from unpaced work, where operatives have an opportunity to plan and sequence their work, to that of paced work, would be expected to lower morale and limit the responsibility an operative might have in his job. Herzberg points out however, that an interesting phenomenon takes place. Bewilderment is experienced in the transitional change-over period, but the ability of operatives to adjust and accustom themselves to the new conditions, leads them to feel that they have greater responsibility and control over the process and this can lead to higher morale.

participation

An example taken from maintenance work in a chemical manufacturing company and quoted by Davis[89], shows that a redesign of the work organisation and grouped skills led to considerable changes in both the quality and cost of performance. Skills used by general maintenance workers were regrouped across boundaries which had previously caused demarcation problems. Thus the fitter and welder were trained in general welding, layout and fabrication pipe fitting, boiler making, equipment installation and repair.

The result of a broader grouping of skills, introduced by planned cycles of 'on and off' the job training, over about two years and preceded by a reorganisation of the planning department, was to create a rise, followed by a steady decline in costs after the introduction of the new job structures. Direct labour costs fell to below the national index average and 40% below the budgeted costs for the year. There had been a reduction in manning amounting to 42% over a three year period, 1956 to 1959, yet quality, plant utilisation and productivity rose to high levels and maintained these over the same period.

Demarcation problems are well known, for example, four craftsmen—joiner, driller, fitter and caulker—fitting a cabin door stop. Yet shipbuilding demarcation problems only magnify a situation that exists in other industries and in municipal authority maintenance departments. Fitting plaster-board ceilings appears to bear no relationship to the traditional skill of plastering, but in some areas plasterers achieve 'custom and practice' rights while in others joiners carry out this work. It often depends on the relative strengths of the trade unions in the locality.

One of the objectives of productivity bargaining is to encourage fluidity between skills and occupations. Observe however, that in order to introduce an effective change, retraining needs to be undertaken and skills grouped into appropriate combinations. A dangerous situation arises for the industry which ignores technical advance and allows skills to ossify. This also applies to companies implementing productivity agreements where flexibility of labour has been agreed, but who have not given much consideration to programmes of retraining or designing appropriate skill combinations.

In the building maintenance survey, it was observed that where mechanical, electrical and building sections were each under the control of a senior engineer; demarcation inhibited fluidity between skills and as a result a highly sophisticated document flow and costing system was necessary to maintain reasonable communication and control.

Answers received to the question: 'What particular things do you dislike about your job?' were, in the majority of cases, directed at the organisation of work and administrative procedures. The most regular comments being:—'too much paper work—too much red tape—the way things are run—we get messed about—the organisation is not progressive enough—disorganisation—no room for initiative on the workman's side'.

Where the mechanical and electrical sections were both under the control of one senior engineer, the borderlines between the skills were more fluid than were the borderlines between the building section and the other two. Furthermore, in the smaller organisations where all sections were under the control of one engineer, the fluidity between appropriate skills and combinations ranged far and wide. The administrative communications and costing systems were seen to be very simple and effective in these cases.

There is a need for efficiency in the design of work organisations but it must be recognised that effective motivation contributes to this efficiency and that certain job satisfactions must be permitted. For example, job scheduling which lays down exactly the order in which jobs shall be performed is necessary in some mechanised and paced situations, but if adopted for other situations removes a freedom of choice from the worker, which does nothing to improve the control of the work and only prevents him from using his opportunity for choice. Maintenance for instance can be scheduled and yet it has been mentioned that a maintenance worker likes to use his initiative and this can still be arranged by giving him an opportunity to select his own order of carrying out the jobs over a period of two or three days.

Workers themselves like to have a voice in the decisions that affect them, they want to be treated as individual human beings, rather than as an undifferentiated mass. There is a movement to promote more consultative practices within industry, where it is envisaged that workers through their representatives can participate in decision making, even to the extent of policy making. Whether this will provide motivation and job satisfaction is yet to be seen.

Different work situations require different treatments which are constantly changing as a result of internal or external influences. From the relatively small amount of research in the field of motivation the indications are that a worker does seek more than monetary reward from his job, but to obtain the best effect and relationship between man and his job, job design and selection procedures must become more orientated towards 'satisfiers' rather than dependent upon customs and traditions.

Chapter 14

Methods of Payment

Before examining the virtues of incentive payment systems, it is necessary to comment upon the methods of payment adopted by the engineering industry.

National minimum wage levels are negotiated between the Engineering Employers Federation and the Confederation of Shipbuilding and Engineering Unions. Where facilities exist, non-federated firms generally follow suit by negotiating with worker representatives at plant level and often settle in advance of the federated agreements by forecasting the outcome of national negotiations.

There are two principal methods of payment:

(1) Timework
(2) Payment by results

From December 1969 the national minimum time rate agreed for a skilled fitter is £15·00 per 40 hour week, and this will progressively increase—as the result of a second long term agreement, dated December 1968—to:

Table 14.1

Date New Minimum Rates to be Effective	Time Rate £
December 1970	17·50
December 1971	19·00

In all cases the time rate of the worker concerned will be guaranteed irrespective of supplementary earnings.

In payment by results systems, piecework prices and bonuses are fixed domestically by mutual arrangement and should enable a worker of average ability to earn at least 15% over the prevailing time rate. Once established the piecework price may not be altered, unless:

(1) there is a mistake in the calculation by either party
(2) the material, means of production or quantities are changed, provided that the modification is such as it will effect a reduction in earnings of the workers concerned
(3) a mutual arrangement has been made between the employer and the worker, in the same manner as a new price is arranged.

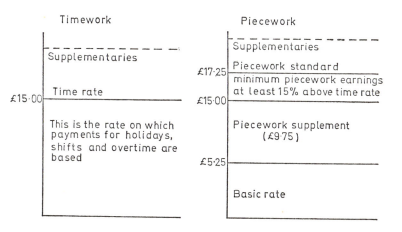

Figure 14.1

Figure 14.1 by using the fitter's rates as an example, attempts to illustrate the simplicities (or complexities whichever the case may be) of the payment methods based on the second long term agreement of December 1968.

The term 'Time Rate' in the agreements is synonymous to 'Consolidated Time Rate' the word 'consolidated' being now outmoded.

The new piecework standard should be at least 15% above the time rate for the appropriate class of worker, and the piecework prices should be arranged so as to enable a worker of average ability to earn this amount without undue exertion. For example, in the case of the fitter rated as national minimum level, the new piecework standard should be £15·00 plus 15% of the time rate (£2·25) thus equalling £17·25.

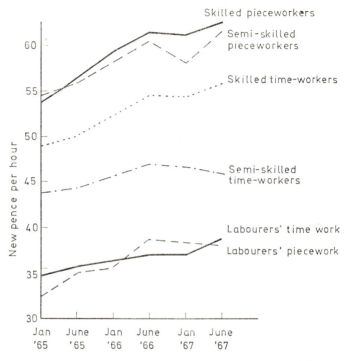

Figure 14.2 *Earnings Differentials—Motor Vehicle Manufacturing Industry*

The new basic rate of £5·25 is determined by subtracting the national piece-work supplement prevailing from the time rate. The piecework supplement made to Payment by Results workers, in addition to piecework earnings, originated as a War Bonus of £0·25 per week paid pro-rata to hours worked, awarded by the Committee of Production in 1917. Various fluctuations occurred to this bonus and in 1943 it stood at £1·78 for Time Workers and £1·67 for P.B.R. workers and in the same year it was redesignated a National Award. By 1950 the bonuses were £2·05 and £1·65 per week respectively. At this time a major change occurred which was to affect all future calculations of methods of payment. By agreement with the trade unions the time workers National Award was consolidated into the time rate which, up until recently, was commonly referred to as Consolidated Time Rate, C.T.R. The major effect of this was to improve the premiums for overtime, holidays and shiftwork which are normally based on the time rate.

The existing National Award was retained for P.B.R. workers as a National Piecework Supplement, and the practice of adding nationally agreed increases to the piecework supplement has continued so that P.B.R. workers receive the same increase as time workers.

Where piecework is the rule however, it will be seen that the bonuses form a large proportion of weekly earnings. In the vehicle industry they are often equal or greater than the basic rate and piecework supplement added together. A view often expressed is that the bonus element is too high to be considered as an incentive to the rate of output, and yet to a minority of Midlands' industrialists, P.B.R. based on ratefixing is the only means whereby the greatest rate of output can be generated.

Nevertheless piecework systems, because of the large bonus element bear little relation to the actual work content—the bonus is simply the result of a power bargain on the shop floor between rate fixers and operatives which provides no adequate measure of security of earnings or of effective management control.

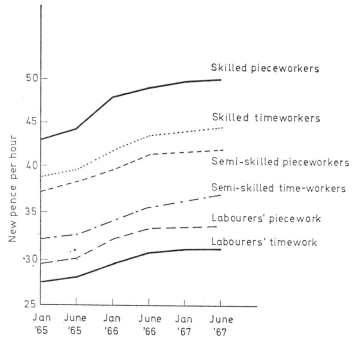

Figure 14.3. *Earnings Differentials—Mechanical Engineering Industry*

118

The problem lies in the fact that pieceworkers earnings tend to rise as a result of numerous changes in component feature bargaining, while time workers, usually the higher skilled, have little opportunity to raise the time rate. Inequalities and anomalies in relative pay are a frequent and recurring consequence of P.B.R. systems, and these in turn set off pressures for other wage adjustments to bring workers who have fallen behind the leading groups back into line.   *Payments by Results.*

The contribution that P.B.R. systems make toward distorting the wage levels and differentials of workers in the mechanical engineering and vehicle industries is illustrated in Figures 14.2 and 14.3 extracted from the N.B.P.I.[90]

14.1 PRESENT TRENDS

It was suggested by Norris[91] in 1963 that: 'the influence of trade unions over the past 20 years has increased the level of earnings and their value in monetary terms'. No doubt they have played an important part for the benefit of their members and improved the general standard of living, but employers and management have been forced to inflate earnings domestically and locally in order to counteract labour shortages, scarcity of skills, and disputed time values. They have managed this by:

(1) paying more than nationally agreed rates (between 1965 and 1968 local wage earnings rose more than twice as fast as national wage rates)
(2) allowing overtime to become a regular practice thus creating a false sense of security in the level of earnings.
(3) providing additional lieu bonuses and other financial and fringe benefits
(4) influencing the manner in which piecework rates are bargained in order to maintain complacency rather than cause dispute

The present high and drifting earnings levels are the result of inadequate bargaining procedures not only at plant level, but nationally. From the workers' point of view it is precisely the wage drift that is responsible for increased earnings. For example Table 14.2 indicates that in vehicle companies between 1957 and 1967 there was much greater increase in P.B.R. as compared with measured daywork earnings. Thus much of the resistance of employees might seem less irrational from their viewpoint than might be primarily supposed.

Table 14.2

	Rate per hour £		Increase £	Increase by National Award £	Increase by Wage Drift £
P.B.R. workers	1957	1967			
Rootes and B.M.C. M.D.W. workers	0·41	0·72	0·34	0·09	0·22
Ford and Vauxhall	0·32	0·48	0·16	0·10	0·06

According to the National Board for Prices and Incomes Report No. 65 much of the blame for the drift must be laid on the foremen and rate fixers who are responsible for negotiating piecework prices. The report states: 'The foremens' loyalty lies more with the men than with the piecework system'. Evidently the foreman often books 'lost time' at the most lucrative compensation rates available, irrespective of the cause of the production hold up. Rewards for a favour, or a good job done, are frequently made by booking lost time when none has been lost.

Under such payment systems, most 'indirects' (apprentice trained craftsmen, maintenance workers, toolroom workers, toolsetters, inspectors, storemen and unskilled people) are dependent upon the 'directs' (the majority of whom are semi-skilled) to bargain and help provide them with a respectable pay packet. Many of the 'indirects' are in favour of P.B.R. for 'direct' employees precisely because it causes a wage drift, thus giving them a lever to press their own wage claims in order to maintain traditional differentials.

I

Chapter 15

Financial Incentive Schemes

When introducing incentive schemes it is important to realise that there are very few short cuts, and none for the beginner. Incentive schemes are the means by which people are encouraged to increase output to standards derived by work measurement. It must be emphasised that there is no substitute for painstaking and comprehensive studies by competent practitioners providing a reliable basis for estimating and control, as well as a basis for payment, in which confidence can be maintained at all levels of the firm. It is also important that direct imitation of other industrial or company schemes and agreements should not occur unless the people who adopt them are fully aware of the behaviour and limitations of such schemes.

15.1 CONTRIBUTION TO PRODUCTIVITY

For those who have mixed feelings and are unsure of the benefits of financial incentives, Norman and Snaith[87] found evidence that financial incentives based on work measurement were not the main or only contributor to higher productivity. In one company it was found that a reorganisation of methods of work resulted in a 22% improvement in output, while the implementation of a financial incentive contributed only 4% improvement.

The researchers base their evidence on data obtained from 'cost code entries' and hours booked between January 1966 and June 1967. Two representative periods were compared—one before the financial incentive scheme commenced (February to June 1966) and one after (February to June 1967). The data were derived from individual daily and weekly time analysis sheets; the latter containing comprehensive details of the number of entries per 'cost code' together with man hours booked on each code. The details also included:

(1) a brief description of the type of work done
(2) the different buildings in which the repairs had been carried out.

Table 15.1 indicates by department, the hours and cost code entries made between January 1966 and June 1967. The 'hours per entry' are repeated in graphical form in Figure 15.1. By com-

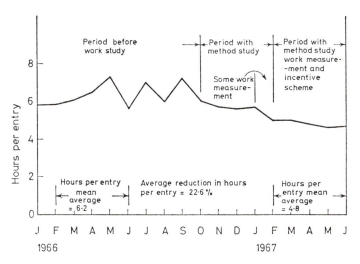

Figure 15.1. *Hours per cost code entry for the period January* 1966 *to June* 1967. *Comparisons are made between February to June* 1966 *and the same period in* 1967

paring the mean average of the 'hours per entry' for February to June 1967 with that of the same period in 1966, a 25% reduction is observed and of this 4% was achieved between February (the commencement of the scheme) and June 1967. Furthermore, following the commencement of the scheme, Figure 15.2 shows a marked trend towards, both, more 'cost code entries per week' and fewer 'hours per entry'. It can be seen that the entries ranged from 316 to 549 in 1966 (including January 1967), while from February to June 1967 'entries' increased markedly, ranging from 591 to 679. At the same time 'hours per entry' in 1966 ranged from 5·6 to 7·3, while from February to June 1967 they reduced markedly ranging from 4·6 to 5·0.

In connection with the trend 'hours per entry' shown in Figures

Table 15.1 NUMBER OF HOURS AND COST CODE ENTRIES BY DEPARTMENT

Month	Building Section			Electrical Section			Mechanical Section			Total for the Department		
	Hours Booked	Entries Made	Hours Per Entry	Hours Booked	Entries Made	Hours per Entry	Hours Booked	Entries Made	Hours per Entry	Hours Booked	Entries Made	Hours per Entry
1966												
Jan.	1130	182	6·2	1402	287	4·8	447	39	11·4	2979	508	5·8
Feb.	1110	174	6·3	1275	283	4·5	644	60	10·7	3029	517	5·8
Mar.	1213	199	6·1	1321	262	5·0	599	59	10·0	3133	520	6·0
April	1160	164	7·0	1433	276	5·2	613	57	10·8	3206	497	6·4
May	861	142	6·0	1337	192	6·9	609	51	12·0	2807	385	7·3
June	945	167	5·6	1294	281	6·0	602	59	10·0	2841	507	5·6
July	970	139	6·9	1324	227	5·8	573	45	12·7	2867	411	7·0
August	909	152	6·0	1213	225	5·3	385	44	8·7	2507	421	6·0
Sept.	758	105	7·2	1028	170	6·0	496	41	12·2	2282	316	7·2
October	919	149	6·1	1263	245	5·1	600	64	9·1	2782	458	6·0
Nov.	889	151	6·0	1224	261	4·7	528	49	10·5	2641	461	5·7
Dec.	1150	170	5·8	1356	295	4·2	600	84	7·1	3106	549	5·6
1967												
Jan.	1138	161	6·1	1394	281	4·8	503	70	7·2	2917	512	5·7
Feb.	911	145	6·3	1408	353	4·0	608	93	6·5	2927	591	5·0
March	948	193	4·8	1201	289	4·2	917	134	6·8	3066	616	5·0
April	991	151	6·3	1191	298	4·0	818	168	4·8	3000	617	4·8
May	1051	197	5·3	1181	336	3·5	901	146	6·1	3133	679	4·6
June	949	199	4·7	1125	274	4·1	821	122	6·4	2895	595	4·8

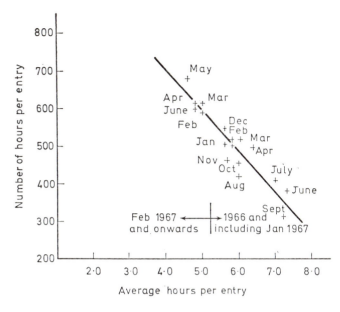

Figure 15.2. Relationship between numbers of hours per entry and average hours per entry

15.1 and 15.2, and immediately prior to the commencement of the financial incentive scheme, the period November 1966 to January 1967 inclusive was a period where both a significant increase in the number of 'cost code entries' and reduced 'hours per entry' occurred as a result of some broad changes that took place in the organisation of work, which were:

(1) a reorganisation of work allocations after management had attended a short course in Work Study
(2) the introduction of provisional times during December 1966
(3) a certain amount of method study prior to the commencement of the scheme.

Table 15.2

	May 1966	*May* 1967	% *Reduction*
Week 1	482 hours	192 hours	60
2	333 ,,	221 ,,	34
3	355 ,,	183 ,,	48
4	344 ,,	156 ,,	55

Because of the desire to change the wage level quickly, the amount of reorganisation carried out was limited to studies of general factors affecting large groups of men, such as:

(1) the inclusion on job cards of precise details of materials and tools required for the job, intended to reduce the number of visits to stores and to cut down waiting time
(2) the grouping of jobs into sectors to reduce changeover and travelling time
(3) the creation of facilities for tea breaks at points nearer the locality of site working than to the canteen.

Following the commencement of the incentive scheme, the researchers calculated that the number of hours worked on overtime had reduced by an average of 50% per week as shown in Table 15.2.

15.2 TYPES OF SCHEME

There are various schemes in general use—some primarily designed to improve productivity by encouraging workers to use their working hours more effectively. However, it is not unfair to suggest that at the time of the last Government's wage restraint several schemes were proposed, not as a means of improving productivity, but with the primary need to raise the level of earnings.

Incentive schemes may be designed for:

(1) Individuals—where a worker's own performance decides the bonus percentage
(2) Group—where the average performance achieved decides the bonus percentage.

To obtain a fair understanding of what is to follow the reader must already be familiar with the terms used in Chapter 4, i.e. the calculation of operator and departmental performance indices —calculations that are fundamental to many incentive schemes based on work measured data, the most popular being:

(1) Straight proportional
(2) Geared
(3) Multi-factor
(4) Measured daywork schemes

Straight Proportional Scheme

Where jobs can be accurately measured and controlled, it is usually considered reasonable to award 33·3% bonus above time work rates to encourage workers co-operation in improving their performances 33·3% above a base level defined by trained work study personnel. For example, as shown in Figure 15.3, when using the B.S. 0/100 rating scale, the employee receives a guaranteed basic wage up to a day rate performance of 75 and thereafter a bonus varying in direct proportion to the output achieved, so that for a 100 performance 33·3% bonus payment will be given. The scheme

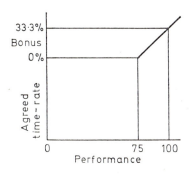

Figure 15.3. *Straight proportional scheme*

is generally accepted as the best financial incentive which lends itself to repetitive work where output is dependent on the operator's own efforts, provided that accurate standard times can be established.

Operator Performance

$$= \frac{\text{Standard Time} \times 100}{\text{Attendance Time} - (\text{Waiting Time} + \text{Diverted Time})}$$

Let T = Time rate
P = Performance

a performance of   75 gives   0% bonus
a performance of 100 gives 33·3% bonus.

Hence each unit step of performance between 75 and 100 earns

$$\frac{1}{25} \text{ of } \frac{T}{3} = \frac{T}{75}$$

Therefore bonus earned $= \frac{T}{75} (P-75).$

Geared Schemes

Certain work such as maintenance is difficult to measure accurately. As a result it is almost impossible to establish a time standard that is representative. Under these circumstances it is desirable to provide an incentive scheme which affords protection to both employer and employee against excessive bonus fluctuations which might occur week by week.

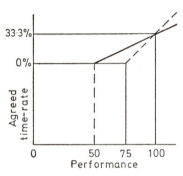

Figure 15.4. Straight line geared scheme

Such a scheme is illustrated in Figure 15.4 where bonus payment begins at a nominal 50 performance (instead of the 75 previously), and rises gradually to the junction of 100 performance and 33·3% bonus.

Above a 100 performance it might be desirable to protect safety and quality standards whereby the angle of slope may be reduced, or even levelled off discouraging employees from unsound work at times when everything appears easy and straightforward.

$$50 \text{ Performance} = \quad 0\% \text{ bonus}$$
$$100 \text{ Performance} = 33·3\% \text{ bonus}$$

Hence, each unit step of performance between 50 and 100 earns

$$\frac{1}{50} \text{ of } \frac{T}{3} = \frac{T}{150}$$

Bonus earned for P performance $= \dfrac{T}{150}(P-50)$

On occasions this scheme is called the $50+\frac{1}{2}$ scheme, which is as follows:

It has already been shown that bonus earned on the straight

proportional scheme at P performance $= T(P-75)/75$. Thus for a corresponding performance of 50/100 on the 75/100 scheme let $P = \mathcal{N}$ (by definition these bonuses are equal)

$$\frac{T}{75}(\mathcal{N}-75) = \frac{T}{150}(P-50)$$

Hence:
$$\mathcal{N} = 50 + \frac{P}{2}$$

This means that for a corresponding performance of 50/100 on the 75/100 scheme, the comparative performance is calculated by adding to 50 one half of the actual performance. For example, if an operative has a performance of 80 on the 50/100 scheme, he would have a comparative performance of $50 + 80/2 = 90$ on the 75/100 scheme.

Hyperbola type Geared Scheme

A geared scheme adopted by several building and plant maintenance organisations is shown as a hyperbola in Figure 15.5.

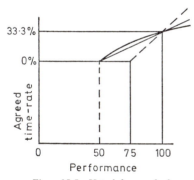

Figure 15.5. Hyperbola geared scheme

Simplicity in calculation is not one of its virtues, and if compared with the straight line geared scheme can be seen to increase unit cost between 50 and 100 performances. This scheme was publicised by Bailey[92] who stated: 'although the hyperbola geared payment curve lacks the simplicity of a straight line geared scheme, it had other virtues which make it particularly suitable for maintenance work'. Two points in its favour are:

(1) that operatives, who have in their experience found incentive

working conditions to be unfavourable, might be persuaded to accept a scheme in which the reward is larger and more immediate for performance between 50 and 100

(2) that management is safeguarded against run-away performance levels over 100 and a cautionary measure is thus introduced to compensate for their inexperience of the effects of incentives and other shortcomings.

It was found in one maintenance organisation that the average departmental performance achieved over the first 10 weeks of operating this type of scheme was 80%. It was calculated that if a straight line geared scheme had been used instead the labour cost would have been considerably less. In this organisation, the group's average performance decided the bonus percentage, i.e.:

$$\text{Group Performance} = \frac{\left[\begin{array}{c}\text{Group Total Standard}\\\text{hours of work completed}\end{array}\right]}{\left[\begin{array}{c}\text{Actual hours of Group}\\\text{taken to complete work}\end{array}\right]}$$

and for the purpose of bonus calculation the original groups in 1966/67 were:

(1) Electricians
(2) Pipefitters
(3) Carpenters
(4) Plumbers, Painters, Bricklayers and Labourers

It was evident as the scheme continued that certain individual operative performances were not as high as expected. For example, older craftsmen maintained an unfavourable attitude towards the scheme and were unwilling to co-operate while the younger craftsmen, eager for higher earnings to meet domestic commitments, were more enthusiastic. However, enthusiasm was short-lived; group average performances were continually being depressed and management were forced to introduce in June 1967, a revised group arrangement.

Table 15.3

Operative Performance Achieved Previous Month	Building Section	Electrical Section	Mechanical Section
90+	Grade 1	Grade 1	Grade 1 only
80 to 90	Grade 2	Grade 2	
80−	Grade 3	Grade 3	

The new groups were arranged into sections and the bonus grades related to specified bands of performance as shown in Table 15.3.

Under the new arrangement a new lease of vitality was injected into the maintenance department. Grade 1 now appeared more attractive to slow workers and their enthusiasm was stirred once more to draw away from the older non co-operative minority.

As the scheme continued it was apparent that a further revision could be of benefit to the organisation. By regrouping the three sections into one (Table 15.4) the scheme would be completely transformed into a 'graded performance scheme', defined in B.S. 3138[39] as: 'A payment by results scheme comprising a series of bonus grades, related to specific bands of performance. Operatives are paid a bonus rate dependent upon their past performance, averaged over an extended period of time, e.g., several weeks or months'.

Table 15.4

Operator Performance Achieved Previous Month	Maintenance Department
120+	Grade 1
110 to 120	,, 2
100 to 110	,, 3
90 to 100	,, 4
90 −	,, 5

To ensure a smooth introduction of the original scheme the management included a 'learner allowance' for a period of eight weeks in order to compensate for unfamiliarity with the scheme.

Multi-Factor Schemes

Other schemes, as described by Norman[36] are not enthusiastically received by employers because of their control complexities, but there are many occasions when physical work is not the best measurement of an operative's contribution to output. For example, where quality becomes more important than speed, and wastage must be controlled, multi-factor schemes are viable propositions, e.g. paint and varnish manufacture.

Two Factor Scheme

Figure 15.6 shows a nomograph of two factors selected to control

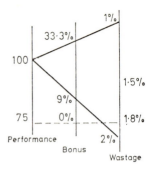

Figure 15.6. Two factor scheme

either quality or wastage, as well as performance. For a performance of 100, a bonus of 33·3% will be paid providing wastage is not more than 1%. Scales are arranged to weight the bonus payable in favour of the most important factor. For example, if a performance of 100 is achieved and a wastage of 2% occurs, a bonus of 9% would be payable instead of the expected 33·3%.

Multiplying Three Factor Scheme

Bonus payment is calculated as a percentage of the performance achieved and multiplied by factors corresponding to the achieved

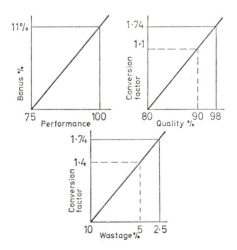

Figure 15.7. Multiplying three factor scheme

quality and wastage performances. Illustrations of this scheme are shown in Figure 15.7. For example:

If performance = 100 = 11% bonus
     quality = 90 = 1·1 conversion factor
   wastage = 5 = 1·4 conversion factor

Therefore bonus payable = 11 × 1·1 × 1·4 = 17%

Measured Day Work

In a working environment a negative incentive can be a positive motivator towards higher performances, but can also result in exploitation, hardship and demoralisation. A balance is essential in any arrangement between management and operatives.

Measured day work is devised on the basis of positive and negative incentives and is defined by 'a system of payment in which an additional fixed award is paid on top of the prevailing time rate. The extent of the award is dependent upon the operative, or operative group meeting a contractual measured standard of performance related to output. It is paid regularly as long as this output is maintained'.

For management, the contract means that the operative will provide an agreed amount of work under a specified method, with specified equipment, in a stated (measured) length of time, for an agreed amount of pay; with a penalty if the minimum level contracted is not maintained over a period of time.

For the operative the management are prepared to pay a high fixed wage for attaining an agreed target, with a penalty if management fail to provide work or equipment as contracted.

Payment is tied to stepped performance levels, and the higher the contractual standard of performance, the higher the level of fixed payment. A penalty is built in if the contractual level is not maintained over an assessed period of time.

Basically, the principles are to assess by means of work measurement, the standard time to perform a job of work and then to establish a progressive scale of fixed wage levels related to performance—not unlike Graded Performance Schemes already referred to in this chapter.

The general view taken by the Engineering Trade Unions is that measured day work is a great potential danger to shop stewards' authority. It undermines the stewards' negotiating power. Scanlon[93] says: 'with piecework you have the man on the shop floor determining how much effort he will give for a given amount of money.

In other words there is a mutually agreed contract between operators and management representatives. Now with the introduction of measured daywork you have a fixed wage and the question is—how much work will you do for that fixed wage'.

Corfield[94] adds: 'it is essential that our shop stewards appreciate what they are giving up when management propose going over to fixed day wages. The loss may not be in earnings capacity. The change may involve a loss of workshop participation and control over the payments system'. Before starting measured day work it is essential that the company has:

(1) a high rate of productivity
(2) work specifications for the job
(3) work standards of performance
(4) effective programming facilities
(5) effective administration
(6) good industrial relations

High Day Rate

High day rate and measured day work are often regarded as identical schemes. A survey on incentive payment systems as carried out in 1966[95] indicated that one manager in four did not know what high day rate was and it was clear that many were confusing it with measured day work. High day rate is defined as a system of payment in which an additional fixed award is paid on top of the prevailing time rate for the class of work, and paid regularly as long as a recognised level of skill and performance is maintained. The emphasis is on 'recognised' where as in measured day work the extent of the award is dependent upon a contractual measured standard of performance related to output.

From this it can be gathered that high day rate does not give any indication of performance levels nor does it lend itself to a utilisation productivity index. From the survey it was shown that one third of the companies using high day rate thought it useful, one third partially successful and the remainder considered it to be ineffective. The comments of dissatisfaction were:

(1) loses incentive value
(2) supervision has to be maintained at a high level
(3) a chance for shirkers to get away with it
(4) reduces mobility of labour

The survey was designed to find what proportion of the working force was paid on incentives, the type of incentive scheme and the basis on which the incentive was computed. It indicated that five sixths of industry uses some form of incentive scheme and at least one third of this proportion are based on false values as a result of unorthodox measurement or no measurement at all. More than two hundred companies supplied information and of those 65% had adopted time study and 40% favoured synthesis for the basis of the scheme. The surprising fact was that few firms recognised the value of using the post war techniques of Rated-Activity Sampling (14%) and Pre-determined Motion Time Systems—P.M.T.S. (5%).

A more serious aspect however was that 47% of the firms using incentives had no basis of computation and paid bonus on a lieu basis. Ratefixing despite all its shortcomings, is still popular since one third of the firms used it as a basis of bonus payment. British industrialists like incentive schemes, irrespective of their bases, since 95% of the firms using them had more than half of the work force on incentives. A large proportion (61%) thought that the schemes they had adopted were satisfactory although 8% complained that they were costly to operate. The remainder considered that they had lost their impact or should be replaced by something else.

There was no particular preference for group or individual type incentive schemes, although half of the firms used both.

Chapter 16

Productivity Bargaining

The Labour Government through their prices and incomes policy of that time emphasised that increases in labour earnings must go together with rises in output per worker, and as a result, productivity bargaining enjoyed a remarkable rise in popularity. However, as already discussed, productivity indices used by industry and those used by government are grossly inadequate and at times completely erratic in interpreting productivity gains.

The rates of pay for hourly paid workers are generally settled by means of collective bargaining at plant and/or national level. The resultant rates, although endeavouring to maintain differentials between occupational groups and skills, do not necessarily reflect the individual skill and intensity of utilisation required by different jobs, but rather the relative strengths of the bargaining parties at a given time.

Some firms have already found that bonus schemes based on measured performance alone, are already losing their relevance and higher output achievements. Where ratefixing and work measurement have been used mainly as a means of deciding wage levels, some companies now recognise that the time values have a bearing more on wage bargaining than on work content. These companies have experienced that semi-skilled low value work pays higher bonuses under payment-by-results systems, than skilled high value type of work, and therefore its continued use on the increasing number of jobs in which there is less relation between output value and effort value is distorting the wage structure. This does not in anyway imply that method study and work measurement assignments should be discontinued. On the contrary, their application towards 'well-defined' production methods, decision and control, utilisation of facilities and personnel and the improvement of working conditions, are essential without leading necessarily to the bases for bonus payments.

The trade unions have felt obliged to bargain away their customs and practices because it presents a possibility of breaking through government and industrial wage restraints. Nevertheless, in their quest for more money they have spent little time on the actual enforcement of the agreements. As management have gained more effective control over the performance of work, the unions have agreed to bargains that continually attempt to broaden traditional craft boundaries; and include penal clauses such as the 'No Strike No Lockout' clause built into the Henry Wiggin agreement of 1967, which states: 'The employee shall not take part in, call, encourage, support, or give financial or other assistance to any strike, work stoppage, go slow, overtime ban or boycott, among any of the company's employees or any other action directed at interfering with the company's business; and the Company will not lockout the employee'. What is more surprising, they have frequently let slip the opportunity to gain an effective domestic consultation structure giving powers to review wage levels in order to keep abreast of inflation.

In comparing the total weekly earnings of workers, the Donovan Commission in 1968 revealed that of eight local firms examined only two companies had lower earnings per employee than those of the pioneers of productivity agreements, Esso Petroleum employees. In the Electricity Industry, too, the initial large wage gains of the 1965 productivity agreement have since been overtaken by other industries. Apparently the initial agreements sought to base wage reviews on productivity only, failing to realise the effect of price inflation. This tends to substantiate the unions view that higher dividends arise from P.B.R. rather than other review methods or systems of payment.

Productivity bargaining aims for far more than the achievement of higher performances and a mere promise of greater manual effort. A productivity agreement, according to the N.B.P.I. report[96] is: 'one in which workers (through their representatives), agree to make a change, or number of changes in working practice that will make a direct contribution towards economical working, and in return, the employer agrees to provide a higher level of pay, or other benefits. Such agreements can be comprehensive and affect all, or nearly all the manual workers in a company; or they can be partial, normally affecting one practice and a single group of workers'. In fact the N.B.P.I. sees the operation of productivity bargaining as a method of reviewing the whole structure of plant bargaining and providing a more positive means of co-operation

K

between unions and employers as well as increased efficiency.
Flanders[97] correctly maintains, that only the comprehensive type
are influential enough to be regarded as an improvement in work
distribution and relations. He rejects partial productivity bargains
as 'soft options' for management, since they make no demands to
task them with a study of all work categories, but only provides
them with complacency and excuses for the time being. Such
bargains are liable to create new inequalities in wage payment
structures. In agreement Dewdney[98] states: 'The true productivity
bargain is one that looks at a labour force, together with the factory
operation as a whole, and is as ready to develop new systems of
production control, the deskilling of manufacturing methods, new
shop layouts, new storekeeping procedures and new accounting
methods, as it is to debate with shop stewards the lines of demarcation between craftsmen and between maintenance workers and
operatives. The package ought to be looked at as a whole'.

In order to improve the rate of generating added value and
ultimately the fortunes of the company, a productivity agreement
should preferably be comprehensive and aimed at removing waste-
ful energy and non productive work. Considerable evidence is
available where management willingly accept low capacity utilisation, manhandling techniques, bad layouts, restrictive costing
procedures and inflexible communications systems; all of which
contribute to the cost of products, but little to their value.

Added value AV, is the value that a company adds to its products
in time and progress between raw material and finished articles
ready for despatch. In a simplified form, it is the total sales value S,
less the cost of external purchases X, which includes: materials,
consumable items and tools, contracted work, packing, supplies,
fuel power and water, etc.

$$S - X = AV \text{ or Net Output}$$

AV is the income a company must achieve to pay for such items as:

(1) Personnel, benefits and taxes
(2) Sales and marketing
(3) Research and development
(4) Revenue tax, reserves and dividends
(5) Replacement and depreciation of plant and facilities

As added value affects all within the enterprise, all must contribute
towards it and therefore, it is considered only right that the objectives of a productivity bargain should be directed towards all grades,
from managing director to unskilled worker. The principles for
such an agreement would be based upon:

(1) Security
(2) Evaluation—in order to stabilise earnings
(3) Fortunes of the enterprise—the rate of generating added value
(4) Performance—directly provided by an individual or group of employees

In return the objectives should aim to task:

(1) Directors—those who decide company policy.
(2) Management—those who carry out the policy decisions, to study the systems and the pattern of communication within the whole enterprise, and to change working practices that have been considered to be sacred; especially customs and traditions that restrict both growth and the rate of generating added value.

Of those agreements already made each have aimed for various objectives, such as:

(1) A reduction in overtime
(2) A free interchange of tasks between different groups of workers
(3) The removal of restrictions on output
(4) Investment in technological improvements and advanced equipment
(5) Manpower reductions (with the aid of a voluntary separation scheme where necessary)
(6) Changes in patterns of work
(7) Introducing, or continuing the use of method study, work measurement and other management techniques, with or without leading necessarily to direct incentive payments
(8) To compensate with changes in levels and structures pay, of or other benefits such as time off in lieu, improved fringe benefits

A research paper[99] views productivity bargaining as manpower utilisation techniques, which implies that productivity is entirely dependant upon labour. Utilising manpower does not necessarily mean that the company's assets are utilised in the same way, or that the organisation and management systems can absorb the inevitable changes. For example, as the rate of generating output is accelerated so the product mix will change with consequent effect on the degree of planning and control required. There is ample evidence that management organisation and administrative technique which this requires on the part of supervisors, line and staff management and services, has not been forthcoming and it is obvious that more training and education is needed before a company, undergoing productivity bargaining, can be capable of supporting large increases in work loading and related procedures. Company organisations who have experienced the intensity of utilisation that can arise from P.B.R. schemes, are more readily able to accept the changes, but to gain agreement for such changes the compensation in the form of levels and structures of pay and other benefits will be high, simply because of the existing high P.B.R. earnings level.

It must be emphasised that productivity agreements are not the panacea of all incentive schemes, they are only able to assist in bringing about changes in working practice that previously were recognised as firmly established customs and traditions.

When considering a productivity agreement, it is first advisable to recognise the difference between such an agreement and the orthodox type of agreement on minimum rates of pay and conditions.

The ways in which a productivity agreement differ may be:

(1) it is designed for only one organisation
(2) it requires specific undertakings from both sides
(3) it has to deal in detail and comprehensively with matters of working methods, procedures and performances

The objectives of a productivity bargain can only be forthcoming after a preliminary survey has been carried out in the companies contemplating an agreement. The indications, as experienced in other companies, point to the need to incorporate into any changes affecting the labour force, measures to cater for the effects these changes will have on the adjoining branches of the organisation, and it is suggested that all concerned in the organisation should be notified of the preparation for a productivity agreement. The notification should outline broadly the objectives, guarantees and length of time the investigation will take, and the methods for collecting the information on which the agreement will be based.

The procedures needing investigation would include:

(1) communications, grade and responsibilities of each employee
(2) methods of production, planning, control
(3) type of work done and equipment used
(4) content of jobs, time taken, customs and practices
(5) job descriptions and job specifications
(6) working policy and arrangements, overtime and fluctuations in work load
(7) method of payment, and comparison with other local and national rates of pay

(8) costing system, methods of allocating overheads and pricing of jobs.

The research, analysis, bargaining and implementation are processes that must be carried out with care preferably by experts engaged external to the company, assisted by one or more senior managers.
Information arising from the investigation should be studied jointly by the consultants and the co-ordinators to determine:

(1) the principles and objectives
(2) changes in the organisation and system that might be necessary
(3) the phases of implementation

A draft statement on the proposed productivity agreement should be drawn up, detailing:

(1) why this investigation took place
(2) objectives and any necessary guarantees
(3) timing and implementation of each phase
(4) value of increased benefits, financial and fringe
(5) changes in patterns of work
(6) continued application of management techniques, method study and work measurement, without necessarily leading to financial incentives
(7) anticipated results of the agreement

16.1 ACTUAL AGREEMENTS

Investigations of labour productivity as defined by those agreements already made, began in 1958 at the Esso Fawley Oil Refinery; comprehensively discussed by Flanders.[97]

A number of firmly established customs and traditions were to be challenged before the agreement of 1962 was finally settled.

The original objectives were to:

(1) reduce overtime over a period of two years, from the 1959 average of 18% to 6% per annum for process work and to 2% per annum for maintenance work
(2) encourage fluidity between craft skills within similar working groups and to transfer craftsmen's mates into occupations more suited to their abilities and to the value of the company; some to perform skilled work, and the remainder trained to do other work at the refinery

(3) permit process workers to carry out some basic craft maintenance jobs of low skill content

(4) introduce temporary shift working and to eliminate tea breaks and other contributory unproductive time allowances

At the same time the management took an opportunity to reorganise the supervisory structure. In return, the company promised that no employee would be made redundant as a result of any agreement on these proposals. It was expected that work would be transferred from contract labour to direct labour as the refinery continued to expand.

Discussions continued to establish further flexibility of working procedures and fresh agreements were made in January 1963 and October 1964, although in both these instances, wage settlements were finalised by collective bargaining.

By 1962, overtime had reduced to an average of 11% per annum for process work and to 4% for maintenance and was claimed to be under the control of management. By 1964 however, it was evident that the demand had not increased as forecasted and a voluntary separation scheme was agreed with the trade unions. Of some 400 employees who volunteered to leave, 80 were process workers and the remainder mostly semi-skilled employees.

Since the voluntary separation scheme, overtime rose, and in 1966, achieved an average of 15% per annum for process work and 10% per annum for maintenance and construction work. The reasons given by the company for this increase were:

(1) a plague of fires and breakdowns

(2) an unexpected loss of process workers under the voluntary separation scheme

(3) an unwillingness to recruit because of uncertainty in demand and investment prospects

To obtain agreement in the 1962 proposals, the company agreed to increase the basic wage by 40% of the original over a two year period. For daywork craftsmen this amounted to: £0·3 per hour, in April 1960 rising to £0·42 per hour by April 1962. A shift allowance of £0·11 per hour was also given. Since the published agreement, further wage settlements have been made: £0·49 per hour in April 1964 rising to £0·59 per hour by April 1967 by normal plant bargaining procedures.

Although the Fawley agreement was the forerunner of many similar agreements there were significant differences in the way each company defined their objectives.

Esso Milford Haven Refinery began their investigation in 1962, and presented the proposals for consideration in the Summer of 1964. The agreement, however, was delayed until September 1965 before it was made final and unanimously accepted.

Milford Haven is a highly capitalised plant supported by a direct labour force of some 70 process workers and 50 maintenance workers.

The objectives of the agreement in this instance were aimed to:

(1) encourage fluidity between craft skills and process workers to the extent that process workers were trained in individual basic maintenance tasks, and craftsmen were to provide cover for process workers and to undertake process jobs

(2) reorganise the maintenance and process departments into one operations department and to reduce supervision at the same time improving standards

Before the agreement, craftsmen refused to be supervised by process supervisors no matter how urgent the work. This barrier has now been removed. The wage rates for daywork craftsmen ultimately increased by an average of 23% over two years, from £0·45 per hour in April 1965 to £0·55 per hour in April 1967.

Plant maintenance in most capital intensive companies is an underrated problem. No matter how flexible the labour, unplanned emergency repairs are often carried out under the urgency of keeping production down-time to a minimum. Patching and unreliable repairs are encouraged and rarely is an effort made to analyse and correct the real cause of failure. The productivity agreement of Milford Haven, supported by a controlled planned maintenance system is vital to all similarly invested companies.

Another Esso agreement was made final in the distribution services organisation in January 1966 where something like 1 500 drivers and mates together with 2 350 services personnel were directly concerned in improving productivity, and the objectives of this agreement were to:

(1) reduce overtime from 28% to an average of 5% per annum

(2) encourage drivers to load their vehicles, drive without mates and give quicker vehicle turn-rounds. Larger vehicles were introduced under the same proposals

(3) extend the 30 mile/h speed limit to the new legal limit of 40 mile/h

(4) change the pattern of shift working by reducing shift hours from 5 shifts of 11 hours per week to 5 shifts of 8 hours per week, with overtime reserved for emergencies only

(5) encourage the use of work measurement and 'tachographs'

(a time recorder to measure running time of a vehicle along with other activities)

The accompanying increase in wage rate was originally planned to be introduced in four phases spread over 18 months, but had to be finally rephased into a 45% increase inside 8 months. The rate per hour increased from £0·36 per hour in April 1966 to £0·52 per hour in April 1967.

The Imperial Chemical Industries (I.C.I.) recognised as one of the pioneers of the application of work study in Britain and of financial incentives based on 'standard minute' performances, found that there were deficiencies in their existing working practices which created inequalities between output-value and effort-value. They have experienced that semi-skilled 'low value' jobs paid higher bonuses than skilled 'high value' jobs, and the continued application of such schemes was distorting the pay structure.

Proposals of changes in working practice involving 66 000 employees out of a total labour force of 115 000 were first presented to the trade unions in April 1965. The objectives were to provide greater fluidity between craft skills and process work.

(1) allow process workers, with suitable training, to carry out basic craft maintenance work of low skill content
(2) encourage craftsmen to operate process plants when the occasion demands
(3) encourage craftsmen to take orders and requests for work from general supervision of any background experience
(4) encourage craftsmen to do the work of other occupations which form a subsidiary part of the main occupation
(5) allow the use of craftsmen, semi-skilled or general workers to support other craftsmen when the occasion demands

As compensation for these changes each worker was placed on one of the 8 annual salary levels ranging from £760 for Grade 1 to £1 250 for Grade 8, determined by job evaluation.

A productivity and status agreement was made in December 1966 in the Electricity Supply Industry, affecting 155 000 manual workers employed by the C.E.G.B. and 12 Area Boards. The objectives aimed for in this case were to:

(1) reduce overtime from an average of 51 hours per week to that of a normal working week allowing 'blue collar' workers to enjoy social status and benefits with those of clerical, technical and administrative personnel
(2) utilise mates more effectively by pooling their numbers, and encourage slight advantages in intercraft flexibility

(3) change patterns of shift working to meet consumer peak periods

Shortly after its introduction, the Chairman of the Electricity Council remarked that it was too early to form any general opinion of the industrial staff's reactions. Many had been used to working long hours of overtime and found that increased leisure time was poor compensation for the loss in overtime earnings. Nevertheless, he thought that the employees were coming to terms with the new working arrangements.

It is important to realise that pooling of personnel without some additional motivation, can result in operatives delaying their changeover time between one job and another. Evidence of this happening in companies using similar methods emphasises the importance of well defined production planning and resource allocation procedures, with the additional support of direct financial incentives.

An entirely new approach to productivity bargains emerged in January 1968 when a non federated company prepared a two phased agreement. The first phase was simply aimed at rationalising and simplifying the wage structure by job evaluation methods. More than fifty varieties of hourly wage rates and bonus levels were categorised into seven grades, and at the same time a general level of improvement was made to earnings. The following objectives were agreed, with the promise that a further development of the wage structure would be negotiated in phase two to complement the phase one agreement:

(1) removal of restrictive practices with regard to new working methods and equipment, leading towards higher quality standards and increased productivity

(2) flexibility of labour to be maintained at its present high level and enhanced whenever beneficial to productivity

(3) establishment of manning and its control determined by work study

(4) productivity committees comprising equally of trade union representatives and management to be set up to identify areas for increased productivity and to ensure implementation of the approved suggestions

The second phase of the agreement was to install a 'Labour Unit Value Index—L.U.V.I.' determined by the added value contributed by the company, and for simplicity converted to an index which is:

$$\text{Labour Unit Value Index} = \frac{\text{Added Value}}{\text{Total Labour Cost}}$$

The basis for calculation is as follows:

Net Sales (after allowances, royalties and cash discounts have been made) $\Big\} = S$

Outside Purchases:
materials
contract service
power
fuel
water
packing and supplies
consumable items and tools

$\left.\begin{array}{l}\\\\\\\\\\\\\end{array}\right\} = X$

Unavoidable Costs:
salaries and benefits
maintenance and depreciation $\Big\} = Cu$

$$S - X - Cu = AVnet$$

Labour Costs (Operators):
all wages including overtime paid to hourly
wage earners (excluding apprentices).
Plus:
the company's contribution to:
national health unemployment insurance
graduated pension fund
company's pension fund
holiday pay (credited monthly)
extra service holiday pay
sick pay

$\left.\begin{array}{l}\\\\\\\\\\\\\\\end{array}\right\} = Cly$

$$\text{Moving Average Index} = \frac{AVnet}{Cly}$$

For the purpose of smoothing sudden fluctuations that might occur monthly, the index is calculated over a three month moving average and applied to the hourly rates as a productivity bonus. It is adjusted up or down according to the index. The company prefers a gap of one month to calculate the bonus and to make any adjustments that might be necessary (Table 16.1).

Table 16.1

Moving Average Index Period	December January February	January February March	February March April
Hourly Productivity Bonus paid out	April	May	June

Although there appears to be some similarities between this scheme and those of Scanlon and Rucker,[100] and with those of the Federated Engineering Company's Agreement,[99] it does go most of the way towards the principles on which a productivity agreement should be based.

Thus, to improve L.U.V.I., labour must be utilised more effectively, by:

(1) reducing waiting time
(2) reducing overtime
(3) increasing flexibility
(4) reducing skilled time on unskilled work
(5) improving methods to reduce the amount of labour per job
(6) reducing absenteeism

If added value is improved by increasing throughout per hour at lower unit cost, everyone gains—L.U.V.I. rises and earnings improve—consequently the customer tends to gain and the company is better able to maintain or improve its competitive ability.

Chapter 17

Job Evaluation

One of the objectives of productivity bargaining is to change the levels and structure of pay, and set comparative wage rates. This is necessary because methods of payment and powers of bargaining have created inflation, not only in relation to output per head, but also in the differentials between skills.

Norris[91] claims: 'People are always comparing their jobs, wages and bonuses, usually to their own detriment. Someone always gets paid more for an easier looking job.' This might be true where comparisons are made within the same working group, but when building maintenance workers were asked to comment upon the earnings of other people in occupations, such as building contract work, automotive industry, agriculture and bus driving, their answers gave no indication that they viewed other occupations with higher or lower wages as being related to themselves. However comparisons will always be made especially when the earnings level is a symptom of dissatisfaction.

Wage structures within industry are complex and inequalities will always be found. Such anomalies will cause discontentment among employees within a single group, between management and employees, and even within the ranks of management. Otis and Leukart[101] say: 'when one worker in a group (of similar skills) obtains a wage advantage over his fellow workers, he soon discovers that he has lost popularity and that his advantage is resented'. There is considerable evidence of this happening, particularly where the remainder of the group have been unsuccessful in their claim for equal rates.

Some craft skills such as toolmakers, patternmakers, plumbers and electricians consider themselves, by tradition, superior to other skills and enjoy the satisfactions of both prestige and top rates of pay.

National and local wage councils recognise this superiority in their establishment of wage rates.

The effect of job evaluation is to reduce the variety of wage levels within a company by collecting together jobs of relative skill, responsibility, effort and conditions, thereby narrowing the earnings differentials of superior craft skills to those of other skills. This, according to Gomberg[102] 'encourages the dilution of the craftsman's skill and is a threat to his status in the work hierarchy.' The truth of this statement was brought home to the management of British Leyland Pressed Steel Fisher Works, at Oxford in April 1968, when Patternmakers and Electricians joined together to dispute the small number of job evaluation grades that were being proposed. With five grades the unskilled and semi-skilled would be able to overtake the Patternmakers and Electricians pay grades; but with seven grades—the Patternmakers and Electricians placed in the seventh—the traditional differentials would be secure. Gomberg went on to conclude: 'If both worker and supervisor agree that, for example, the cementers are the aristocrats of the raincoat industry, what useful purpose is served by upsetting this scale of values in favour of some mechanistic criterion of equity? These traditions are every bit as important as job content.' Nevertheless, traditions are forced to change as production methods are influenced by the product mix, skill and effort content are affected by capital investment and automated techniques.

To consider building a sound and equitable wages structure on the basis of craft skill alone would be unjust, for in the majority of cases it has been shown that traditional craft titles are not always indicative of the occupation being carried out. Norman and Snaith[87] found that of several men classified as Electricians in a building maintenance organisation could more appropriately be classified as Lift Engineers or Domestic Equipment Engineers, both jobs having a considerable mechanical content. A third Electrician was wholly employed on lamp changing—a job more suited to a domestic cleaner.

However, there is evidence that the influence of the overall nature of the job compares with the influence of wage levels. They range from simple repetitive one operation jobs, to those that require many operations, each requiring skill, experience and responsibility. Some jobs are largely physical while others are done under disagreeable working conditions. British Standard 3138[39] defines job evaluation as: 'A generic term covering methods of determining the relative worth of jobs.' More precisely, it is the process of determining on a rather subjective basis the relative current worth of occupations analysed in terms of:

(1) acquired skills and knowledge
(2) responsibilities and mental demands
(3) physical demands
(4) working conditions

Its objectives are to:

(1) enable management to build a sound and equitable wage structure (although Gomberg in putting forward a trade unionists view, is not so sure that they mean it)
(2) provide information to aid management in wage negotiation, recruitment, training and personnel grading, and indirectly to improve working conditions

Mortimer[103] says: job evaluation has many advantages. 'It compels management to take a disciplined approach towards staffing problems. It wrenches them away from traditional but lazy habits of thought in relation to the need for skilled workers.' It does not achieve an absolute reward as this depends upon a variety of conditions unrelated to the job, determined by company policy, monetary value and market economy. Its success depends upon the personalities and skills of the assessors, and it may be desirable to engage established management consultants assisted by one or more senior managers within the organisation. Alternatively where the assessment is to be carried out internally, an evaluation committee would provide the most reliable assessment. The committee members might be drawn from Personnel, Process, Administration, Industrial Engineering and representatives of the major Trade Unions within the company.

The International Labour Office[104] points out: 'comparisons are less easy between broad groups of managerial, clerical, and manual jobs, than between jobs within each of these groups; between different departments than within a given department; and between work crews than within a single crew'.

It is important to note that direct imitation of one company's job evaluation system by another will destroy the foundations of impartial judgement and therefore must be discouraged.

Finally, the views put forth by workers' members of a sub-committee reporting on job evaluation methods in the metal trades, conclude that job evaluation would not promote industrial harmony —'there is a tendency to limit collective bargaining and to freeze the wage structure. Contrary to this, the views of management are that it does not undermine the system of collective bargaining nor the work of the wages councils, for evidence is plentiful particularly in large chemical organisations and government establishments which support the management view'.

In the preparatory stages it is essential that all personnel concerned should be notified, outlining the objectives, guarantees regarding changes, the time the evaluation will take and the manner of collecting the information.

Familiarity must be made with the merits of job evaluation schemes. All types must be considered for their suitability and economic justification in a particular working situation.

A thorough investigation must be carried out, for the analysis of the job should be complete and accurate. Knowledge of the following will help towards an accurate assessment:

(1) employee attitudes towards job satisfaction
(2) utilisation of capital and labour (technical capacities and skill abilities respectively)
(3) communication pattern, grade and responsibilities of each person and to whom responsible. Amount of initiative and ingenuity required
(4) methods of planning, loading and control. Quality standards
(5) type of work done, product mix, methods applied, equipment used and value of equipment. Skills, occupations and number employed on each task. Conditions of work, safety, hazards, etc.
(6) content of job, duration of cycle time and throughput time
(7) working policy, traditions and customs, amount of overtime and methods of payment
(8) comparison of wage and salary rates to local and national rates
(9) fluctuation and seasonal changes in workload
(10) fortunes of the company
(11) experience, training and development
(12) costing and budgeting methods and method of pricing jobs
(13) amount of contract work and other areas from which work can be drawn
(14) stockholding and inventory controlling policies

The above information could be obtained in three ways, depending upon the work situation. For instance, short cycle repetitive jobs can be observed, and the details substantiated by questions taken from a check list as shown.

Check List

Job Title: *Department:*
Brief Description of Duties: *Section:*

From whom do you receive orders?
Are you supplied with all the information you require?

What additional information is required?
Is previous training necessary to do the job?
Do you have to plan ahead and for what period?
What materials is it necessary to recognise?
Is the whole of the method predetermined?
Do you exercise powers of judgement?
Must you use your own initiative?
How many different jobs do you do in a week?
Is it necessary for you to memorise facts and figures?
How long did it take you to learn this job?
What equipment do you use?
What materials do you use?
Is it necessary for you to find faults and make repairs or adjustments?
What is the most difficult part of your job?
What decisions do you make?
Do you perform jobs which have not been done previously?
Are your instructions spoken?
Do you work from drawings?
What calculations do you make?
What writing is necessary?
Is any special knowledge required?
For what materials are you responsible?
What is the value of the materials?
When is your work inspected?
What damage to equipment can occur through negligence?
What is the approximate value of the equipment you use?
Could poor work be received by the customer?
Do you use confidential information?
Do you have contact with outside visitors or customers?
Do you work as a member of a team or group?
Are others responsible to you? If so, how many?
Is it necessary for you to teach others your job?
Are you responsible for others?
What special care is necessary?
What injury could you cause to others?
What is the maximum weight lifted?
How high and how often?
Is equipment provided for lifting and transporting?
Must you keep up with a machine or others?
Is it necessary to work at the same pace throughout the shift?
What is the normal working posture?
In what way is your working posture awkward?
Is agility required?

What type of lighting do you work under?
Does your work require close visual attention?
Do you experience any glare?
Do you continually have to watch several details?
Upon what part of the job must you concentrate?
What information must you memorise?
Do you make unprecedented actions or decisions?
Do you receive several pieces of information at one time from which you must take action?
Do you change your job intermittently or regularly?
Do you take defined amounts of relaxation?
Where do you work?
Is it hot, cold, wet, noisy, dusty, gaseous or toxic?
Do you work higher than ground level or floor level?
What manner of access is there to your job?
Do you work underground?
Is your department crowded?
Is the ventilation good?
Is the heating arrangement suitable for all seasons?
Do you work in a fixed location?
Is there any risk to your health?
What tools is it necessary to supply?
Do you wear special clothing?
Are showers and washing facilities provided?
Are there any special features which have not been considered?
What type of tea break and lunch facilities are provided?

To collect more details an interview could be given to the job supervisor, line manager and to other employees engaged in some part of the job being evaluated.

Long cycle work, particularly varied and occasional jobs, as found in construction, maintenance and toolroom work will require careful consideration. Observation can still be carried out but it must be accepted that details will be missed. The most reliable information will only emerge by direct questioning and interviews.

Analysis of this information should lead to an accurate job description and specification. Smythe and Murphy[105] point out: 'Management literature abounds with discussions of job descriptions and job specifications as though they were entirely separate and disassociated items. The narrow interpretation is that the job description describes only the job, while the job specification specifies merely the type of person required for the job. Actually, a thorough job description includes the cardinal characteristics of the job specification.' A job specification is required to aid Labour Officers

L

and Personnel Interviewers to determine whether or not the appli-
cant under consideration is qualified and experienced to fill the
position. An example of a job specification and job description
follows:

Job Specification

A Works Laundry Driver/Collector is required to carry out the
duties of collecting and delivering clothing supplied by the company
and worn by employees. This is a new post established by work
study investigation.

Department: Transport
Section: Driving
Job Title: Laundry Driver/Collector

The employee must be:

(1) in possession of a current driving licence
(2) experienced in driving 25 cwt. vans
(3) able to carry out daily inspection of vehicles and report on
    defects
(4) of reasonable intelligence, reliable and trustworthy
(5) medically fit
(6) able to handle 80 lb bags of clothing (dry weight) over
    walking distances of approximately 30 yds
(7) knowledgeable of the procedure for monitoring clothing
    suspected of being contaminated and radioactive
(8) able to change his programme to suit demand
(9) able to do other transport duties

Job Description

British Standard 3138 defines job description as: 'A statement of
the content and requirement of a job'.

Job Description No. WA/57
Department: Transport
Section: Driving
Job Title: Laundry Driver/Collector

The Laundry Driver/Collector drives a Bedford 25 cwt. van, and
is responsible for the collection and delivery of laundry throughout

the chemical works. This involves handling upwards of 20 000 lbs of dry laundry per day made up in bags which weigh upwards of 60 lbs but less than 80 lbs when full.

The duties are as follows:

(1) at commencement of duty check vehicle for road-worthiness and report any defects
(2) fill up with fuel, oil and water; check tyre pressures and ensure vehicle is properly equipped with tools and spare wheel
(3) ensure there is a log sheet and enter up as laid down in works instructions
(4) load, deliver and unload clean laundry to specified buildings throughout the works
(5) load, deliver and unload dirty laundry from buildings throughout the works to laundry
(6) ensure outside of bags have been certified clear of contamination
(7) drive vehicle in a manner laid down by law and works instructions
(8) when not employed on the above duties he will be employed as a normal works transport driver

Type of Man required to do the Job

Must be a steady reliable man who can be trusted to work on his own. He requires initiative to meet fluctuations in the quantity of laundry at the various collecting points. He must be presentable and safety minded.

Training and Skill

Only an experienced transport driver will be recruited for this job. For a new man not familiar with the layout of the Works, it would take upwards of a month to learn the location of the various buildings and become acquainted with the variations in the loads of the laundry.

Physical Requirements

Must have good eyesight and hearing and have been passed

medically fit for driving duties by the Works Medical Officer. Must also be fit to lift heavy loads for a large proportion of his day.

Working Conditions

The work is heavy as he has to handle upwards of 20 000 lbs of laundry a day made up in bags weighing approximately 60 lbs but less than 80 lbs.
Some of the loading and unloading is done in the open and subject to all weather conditions.
A uniform is provided. The work is on days only.

17.3 METHODS OF EVALUATION

The process of comparing one job with another is a matter of judgement which relies almost entirely upon the expertise of the Evaluation Committee. There are several methods of comparison but the four most common to British Industry are:

(1) ranking
(2) classification
(3) factor comparison
(4) points rating

A fifth has been originated recently by Jaques of Brunel University called the 'Time Span of Discretion'.

Ranking

'A method of job evaluation which determines the relative position of each job by comparison with all other jobs. It does not indicate the extent of the difference between jobs at different levels'.[39] It is a simple system but requires the evaluator to be familiar with each job. A précis of the job description is all that is required to rank each whole job in order of relative difficulty and value to the company. The I.L.O. points out that jobs ranked on the basis of incomplete information and without well defined standards might lead to the ranking of the job holder rather than the job.

Norris[91] explains: 'certain jobs in the inspection and foreman category may be more administrative than manual, despite the manual work done as part of the job. These various groups will require ranking separately as it will be impossible to put them all in one scheme without basing the ranks on existing pay scales.' There is evidence of a tendency to be unduly influenced by existing job rates of pay.

A variation is the 'paired comparison' in which a job is compared with every other job and ranked in terms of the number of times it appears more difficult or valuable. This system has often been referred to as 'card sorting', where each job description précis is written on a file card and distributed among the evaluators who rank them in order.

Classification

This method is most suitable for clerical and administrative tasks, where the differentials in responsibilities, occupational hazards and physical effort required are minimised. It is however, often called upon to grade standardised manual jobs for which standard rates of pay can be fixed.

Overall descriptions are prepared for a number of grades before actual job characteristics are examined. A précis description is prepared for each task or occupation and allocated to an appropriate grade. Examples of task grading are shown below.

A Grade. Tasks which require no previous clerical experience; each individual task is either very simple or is closely supervised.

B Grade. Tasks which, because of their simplicity, are carried out in accordance with a limited number of well defined rules after a short period of training (a few weeks); these tasks are closely directed and checked and are carried out in a daily routine covered by a timetable and short period control.

C Grade. Tasks which are routine and follow well defined rules, but which require either experience or a special aptitude and are carried out according to a daily routine covered by a timetable and subject to short period control.

D Grade. Tasks which require considerable experience but only a very limited degree of initiative and which are carried out according to a predetermined procedure and precise rules. The tasks are carried out according to a daily routine which varies but not sufficiently to necessitate any considerable supervision.

E Grade. Tasks which require a significant measure of discretion and initiative, or which require a specialised knowledge and individual responsibility.

F Grade. Tasks which necessitate exercising an extensive measure of responsibility and judgement, or the application of a professional technique.

Examples of Task Gradings

Grade A. Running errands and distributing papers.

Grade B. Typing straightforward documents by simple copying from a clear statement.

Grade C. Taking down in shorthand and transcribing simple matter into statements not involving special layout.

Grade D. Taking down in shorthand and transcribing non routine correspondence and straightforward reports which need careful layout and higher speeds.

Grade E. Private secretarial work of a limited character for an executive, including the taking down of shorthand and the transcription of it, preparing masters for duplication, dealing with the normal correspondence and filing.

Grade F. Private secretarial work in the complete sense for a senior executive.

Whilst this appears straightforward, it is extremely difficult to fit an occupation into one grade. Job responsibilities may be apportioned to one grade, but the content of mental skills may be compared to a different grade. The existing wage rates no doubt influence the evaluators and present problems. The method is non analytical and is not broken down into parts but considered as a whole.

Factor Comparison

As already pointed out it is difficult to contain the work done into one occupational title and yet this must be done before job evaluation techniques can be applied. Within any one company there are a large number of occupational titles supported by a large variety of wage rates. Nevertheless there are a number of jobs within this variety capable of representing a fair day's work for a fair day's pay, and the evaluators select these as key jobs ranging in wage rate from the lowest to the highest.

The International Labour Office[104] says: 'The key jobs should satisfy a number of conditions. First, they should be capable of clear definition and analysis in terms of the factors used. Secondly, they should cover a sufficiently wide range as regards the importance of each factor. Thirdly, when the rates for the key jobs are to be used as the standard for the fixing of wages in other jobs, these rates should be regarded as appropriate by all concerned, and in the case of some jobs should not differ too much from the rates paid for these, or similar jobs in the local employment market. Finally, the key jobs should include jobs covering a sufficiently wide range of pay grades including specifically the lowest and one or more among the highest paid jobs in the plants concerned.' This is very subjective and the basis of Factor Comparison relies almost entirely upon the prevailing wage rates within the district and company at the time of assessment. Thus, the evaluation by comparative means is inclined to be influenced by wage drift and therefore perpetuates existing wage rate inequalities.

However this technique does endeavour to compare one job with another, not as a whole, but under each of five job factors:

(1) mental requirements
(2) physical requirements
(3) responsibilities
(4) acquired skill
(5) environment

Job descriptions are analysed with a view to selecting not less than 10% of the company's occupations as key jobs. Each one is then considered singly under each job factor and apportioned some part of the current rate for the job. For example, consider a Pattern-maker's job having a rate of 75p per hour. It might be decided by the evaluators to apportion the rate to each job factor as follows:

mental requirements	=	15p
physical requirements	=	10p
responsibilities	=	15p
acquired skill	=	30p
environment	=	5p
Total		75p

A scale of monetary values is prepared for each factor and the key jobs are ranked in order of rate apportionment for that factor. The remaining jobs in the company are then compared to the key job scales, factor by factor and ranked in order.

The disadvantages of preparing a scale in monetary terms is that it must be revised each time a national or local wage increase occurs and therefore to avoid this it would be better to prepare the scale as points values. A conversion factor would be necessary to convert the points into monetary terms simply to observe the comparisons with current national and district wage rates. Another disadvantage is that the wage rates for key jobs are presumed to be correct and that all other rates are determined by reference to these.

Points Rating

There are numerous points rating methods, all basically similar. Lyttle[106] describes most of these methods in detail and adds: 'the best practice today conforms to four major characteristics and retains them as headings (job factors) even where further subdivisions are used.' These job factors are chosen so that the job being evaluated can be recognised, defined and assessed in comparison to other jobs, and are most generally selected as:

Acquired skill and knowledge
  (a) education
  (b) training and experience
  (c) initiative and ingenuity

Mental and physical demands
  (a) intensity of concentration
  (b) effort applied

Responsibility
  (a) material or product
  (b) equipment or process
  (c) work of others
  (d) safety of others

Working environment
  (a) conditions of work surroundings
  (b) work location and ergonomic considerations
  (c) unavoidable hazards to health

The layout of these factors appears to indicate equality of importance, but for evaluation purposes it will be found necessary to weight the job factors. For example, the 'acquired skill and knowledge' needed by a job could often be more important than 'working environment', or 'training and experience' or 'work location and ergonomic considerations'. It therefore becomes the responsibility of the evaluators to decide the weighting of each job factor.

One simple assessment is to distribute 100 points among the four job factor headings:

Acquired skill and knowledge—say 50 points

(a) education	10
(b) training and experience	25
(c) initiative and ingenuity	15
total	50

Mental and physical demands—say 10 points

(a) intensity of concentration	5
(b) effort applied	5
total	10

Responsibility—say 30 points

(a) material or product	10
(b) equipment or process	10
(c) work of others	5
(d) safety of others	5
total	30

Working environment—say 10 points

(a) conditions of work surroundings	3
(b) work locations and ergonomic considerations	3
(c) unavoidable hazards to health and injury	4
total	10

Another method is to have each evaluator think of a number and distribute among each job factor, total up and calculate the percentage values appropriate to each factor. Then select the mean average percentage values and use as the points rating.

In order to simplify the assessment of content within a job factor, Points Rating methods generally include 'Degrees of Factors', defined by B.S. 3138 as a numerical value assigned to a defined level of a factor. For example:

Experience: Degree 1 = up to 1 month
Degree 2 = over 1 month and up to 4 months
Degree 3 = over 4 months (and so on)

Smythe and Murphy[105] point out that most points evaluation methods use from four to eight degrees of factor and recommend that 'an even number of degrees be used in the development of a points plan'.

Basically, the selection of factors, definition of degrees and points values involve many arbitrary and subjective elements, even though the evaluation of individual jobs might be more objective than other methods.

17.1 WAGE STRUCTURES

In developing a wage structure it is most important to examine not only the time rates of the job group under investigation, but also the individual components that contribute to an employee's gross earnings. Failure to recognise the proportion of earnings relating to say bonuses and premiums will only aggravate further development of job/earnings relationships.

It is not unfair to say that the final decisions regarding wage rates for each job, or group of similar evaluated jobs, relies heavily

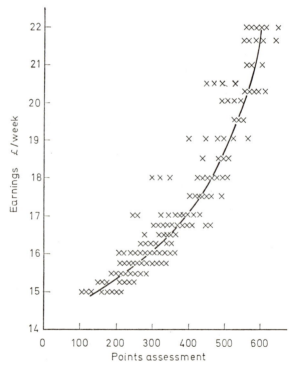

Figure 17.1. *Example of a wage curve*

upon tradition (or occupational title) and bargaining. No matter
how exacting the evaluation might have been, frequent references
are made to current wage levels and wage rates paid for comparable
jobs in other firms and localities. Key jobs, in which a considerable
number of workers are employed and can be sharply defined as
equitably related to one another, are often selected as the basis of a

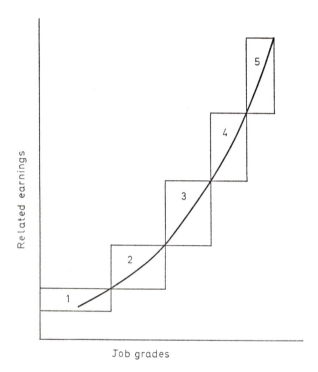

Figure 17.2. Progressive job grades with no overlap

wage structure. Norris[91] prefers to be more thorough in designing
the new wage structure and recommends that each employee's job
evaluated rate should be plotted on a graph of existing wage rates
illustrated in Figure 17.1. Thus ensuring that the existence of
different individual wage rates for the same jobs are accounted for.

With the Points Rating system, understanding of certain traditional and bargaining elements and careful analysis of the wage
curve will indicate the most likely points at which evaluated job
groups can be separated into appropriate grades.

Resistance to the new structure will likely be strongest at these points. If a grade limit is drawn so as to 'separate two occupational groups which have traditionally regarded themselves as equals the result is often conflict'[100] and union demands could quickly destroy the differentials in the job structure.

Nominally five grades are chosen to represent most manual operations in a production environment. However where evaluation schemes overflow into clerical and supervisory work situations, then obviously more grades will be required. High numbers of grades are far more difficult to handle, and it is considered more practical to treat them under separate schemes.

At this stage of development we consider it important to emphasise that the intention of job evaluation is to evaluate the job and not the man. It is essentially concerned with the determination of the appropriate wage rate for the job and as the elements of a job—responsibility, physical and mental requirements, etc., are not likely to change without work study, investment or rearrangement—then there can only be one wage rate. However where it is desired to reward an employee for individual performance, increased responsibility, or long service, the job evaluated rate must be supplemented with other wage components.

One method of constructing an attractive long term wage structure is to combine job evaluation with merit rating by simply grouping the jobs having similar evaluations into labour grades, simultaneously providing a hierarchy of positions and wages within each grade.

There are several ways in which job/earnings relationships may be achieved, two of the most popular being: progression with no overlap (Figure 17.2) and progression with overlap (Figure 17.3). Each grade would have integral merit rating increases where every new employee to the grade would start at the lowest level and progress within the grade.

The progression with no overlap scheme is continually progressive, whereas the overlap scheme allows the longer serving and more responsible person in a lower grade to earn more than a new man in the next higher grade. This allows an employee who reaches the minimum earnings level of the next highest grade to be promoted to the grade for a trial period and if found unsatisfactory can be returned to his previous grade without loss of earnings.

Whichever method is used, there will always be a minority of jobs which appear overpaid or underpaid in relation to others. In such a situation those with low rates for the job grade can simply be promoted. Those whose current wage rates are higher than the maximum established present a more delicate situation and the easiest solution would be to move the occupant onto a job relative

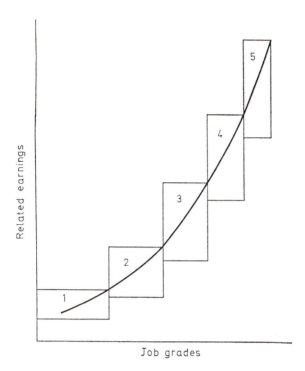

Job grades

Figure 17.3 *Progressive job grades with overlap*

to his current earnings, rather than cause dispute by lowering his earnings to that of the new grade.

An alternative, although undesirable because of the repercussions it might cause, would be to retain the job occupant on his current wage rate until he left the job and then to fill the vacancy at the new wage rate.

Merit Rating

Merit Rating is described as: 'an impartial evaluation of an employee's excellence in matters relating to his present job and to his potentialities for promotion or salary increase'.[39]

Although formal merit rating systems are of recent origin, the rating of employees by supervisors is not a new development. Supervisors often rate the excellence of their subordinates, while they themselves are rated by their superiors. No matter how subjective and unorthodox these ratings might be they are useful in providing some indications of personnel appraisal.

Formalised merit rating is far more discerning, and provides a reliable concept of one individual's excellence compared to another. In the design of such systems it is questionable as to how much emphasis should be placed on merit (excellence in the way a man applies himself to his job) as opposed to length of service. Many companies consider merit in conjunction with service and thereby attempt to provide some element of encouragement to improved excellence, but there are companies who award merit exclusively on length of service which contributes little to the encouragement of improved performance. The practice of paying merit awards annually tends to shift the emphasis from merits of excellence to the length of service factor only.

At one time when the business of manufacturing was not so competitive and complex, merit rating schemes, because of their simplicity seemed to be the most sensible way of rewarding individual effort. Many companies today favour this method in conjunction with job evaluated rates, but those companies who have used it as the only financial incentive to improved performance, many have found it insufficiently flexible to meet the changes taking place in manufacturing methods today.

Some time ago, a non federated company adopted a merit rating scheme in the hope of stabilising earnings and encouraging labour mobility to keep pace with a changing product and process. The scheme was based on merit factors of quality, quantity, attitude to the job, timekeeping and versatility. The advantages aimed for were that employees would:

(1) show more responsibility for their work
(2) show more co-operation and interest
(3) produce less scrap
(4) be more fluid between skilled and semi-skilled work

However, the company was soon to learn that the continuation of the scheme was economically unjustified. They experienced that:

(1) additional supervision was required
(2) overall production time increased
(3) some favouritism was distorting the pattern of rating assessments
(4) the levelling of wage anomalies was taking longer than envisaged

The company decided to replace the scheme with measured day work.

Many other companies have also become aware of uncontrollable weaknesses arising from merit rating. Recently the Ford Motor Company, who have operated such a scheme for the last twenty years, found that the existing three merit grades corresponding to skilled, semi-skilled and unskilled were so broad that jobs of widely varying skill content were all bundled together into the same merit grade, and that almost 80% of the labour force were contained in the semi-skilled group. The scheme had been allowed to ossify in such a way that the borderlines between skilled and semi-skilled had become blurred.

Rating procedures come in many forms and the most popular are:

(1) rank-order systems
(2) paired comparisons
(3) forced distribution
(4) check-list rating systems

While each of the above systems are essentially different in their rating procedures, all are related in that they are developed around merit factors, or behaviour traits.

Rank Order as the name implies, is a system whereby the rater simply ranks his employees in descending order of excellence and allocates a rating relative to his position in rank.

Paired Comparison is a system whereby the rater selects a man who in his judgement is typical of each merit factor and proceeds to pair each ratee with every other one. A rank order emerges where the employee's position once again determines his rating.

Forced Distribution is a method particularly useful for large group appraisals. Nominally, five factors are selected and each is sub-divided into five degrees of merit. A typical rating form is shown in Table 17.1.

An important aspect of this system is to stipulate the percentage of employees to be acceptable under each degree of merit, the idea being to discourage raters from positioning all employees into one part of the scale. The percentages are derived simply to aid the rater in his distribution rather than be used as rigid rules.

Check-list Rating is a system designed around a list of statements that describe the behaviour traits of a specific group of individuals. The traits may range from favourable to unfavourable and for assessment purposes are weighted. It is essential for the system's success that the score should not be common knowledge among raters or their immediate superiors. All that is required of the system is for the rater to indicate one way or another the statements that describe

Table 17.1

EXAMPLE OF AN APPRAISAL USED IN CONJUNCTION WITH THE FORCED DISTRIBUTION SYSTEM

Employees' Name: Department: Grade:

This form is designed to help you appraise accurately the value of employees in the organisation. You are asked to rate the employee on each of several traits or qualities listed. After each trait there is a line representing various degrees of trait. The descriptive phrases beneath the line indicates the amount of degrees of the trait represented by five graduations along the line. They are guide lines. You rate the employee by checking at any place along the line that represents your judgement of him.

						Points Scored
Quality of work	Doubtful that quality is satisfactory	While not unsatisfactory quality is not quite up to standard	Quality is quite satisfactory	Quality of work is superior to that of general run of employees	Exceptionally high quality	
Quantity of work	Unusually high output	Turns out more work than general run of employees	Average satisfactory output	Inclined to be slow	Insufficient output	
Capacity to develop	Future growth doubtful	Moderate development ahead	Shows promise	Very promising promotional material	Great future growth probable, should go far	
Dependability	Unreliable, habitually wastes time	Needs considerable supervision	Requires normal supervision	Can be dependable on most occasions	Thoroughly dependable and steadfast in application	
Attention to safety	Exceptionally careful in every way	Safety conscious	Normally careful but occasionally takes risks	Inclined to be careless	Very careless and a hazard	

the behaviour excellence of each individual, and a senior executive allocates the rating score.

Caution is essential in the use of any system merit rating because all are subjective.[107]

Time Span of Discretion

This method of appraisal is not necessarily job evaluation nor is it merit rating. It assumes that the general worth of a job, or occupation, is determined by the length of time that is allowed for a man to complete a task without receiving instructions from a superior. Time span of discretion is defined as: 'the largest period which can elapse in a role before the manager can be sure that his subordinate has not been exercising marginally substandard discretion continuously in balancing the pace and the quality of his work'.[108] In other words, the discretionary period begins when the employee begins to act upon the task and ends when a superior, or the start of the next stage in the process, checks the results of his action. For example, an assembly worker can have his work passed or rejected by a gauge five minutes after the operation while a managing director can go on until the annual accounts are published. There is a significant correlation between the level of responsibility in the job and the time span of discretion.

To measure the level of discretion in a role, both the occupant and his superior need to be interviewed. What needs to be clarified is whether the role is multiple or single task. If the latter, by sampling the operations within the task, the longest operational sequence can be derived by constructing a sequence chart illustrating the time spans of successive operations and indicating their review points; then extracting the time span of the longest sequence within the task.

In a multiple task role, it will be necessary to derive the task which has the longest target completion time, and by doing so, any routine repetitive tasks, development projects and training requirements need to be noted. The discovery of the time span of discretion in this case will obviously require considerable skill and patience on behalf of the interviewer who needs to be an experienced industrial psychologist. The really difficult case arises where both the role occupant and his superior agree that the work is never reviewed because of the dependability and reliability of the man in the role. In this case, the time can only be derived on the basis of supposition.

The evaluation of wage or salary levels generally emerge in the

M

course of interview. Time span theory claims that within close limits and irrespective of job people having the same time spans of discretion will often state their fair income level.[91] It is held that the fair income level or 'felt-fair' pay is that pay which individuals intuitively feel to be correct for the level of responsibility they are carrying, and further, that at a given level of responsibility the pay which all the different individuals concerned feel they should receive is, within very narrow limits, similar.

By a series of confidential interviews in roles of the same time span, Jaques found that common norms of payment existed which seemed to indicate what differentials in payment are felt to be fair in relation to differentials in level of work.

Chapter 18

Conclusions

Whatever the overriding objective of manufacturing might be, utilising resources of men and machines as efficiently as possible is the most important secondary objective. Here is an identity of interest that needs to be exploited to the full.[109] In general it would appear that labour and manufacturing facilities of all kinds are being grosssly under utilised.

Broadway[110] believes that the nation suffers extensively from capacity shortages and the lack of modernisation investment. On the premise that the West Midlands industries are often looked upon as the nation's 'pace-setters' we found no evidence of capacity shortage. On the contrary, in the firms that were studied (and these were typical), the utilisation of capacity that was available was often only half what it could be.

While the capital investment per employee index did not appear to be significantly different between the West Midlands and the rest of the country, current investment in the region did suggest that the average age of equipment was higher than the national average. Whilst this might adversely affect the productivity index it does not necessarily imply that firms with older equipment are less profitable. Much more critical is the development and advancement of industrial skills, for if a company's production engineering knowledge and practice is inferior, the decision making and control are deficient. In general, industrial managements appear to be only too willing to sacrifice productive utilisation for the convenience of flexibility.

While companies are being urged to employ new techniques and to modernise their equipment, the development of new controlling criteria is urgent, preferably orientated towards facility utilisation. By linking productivity costing indices with those of an effective production planning and control function, it might be possible for the accountant and production manager to work in harmony.

With regard to monetary incentives, the primary objective would appear to be that of increased earnings and not that of improving labour performance. Our evidence shows that where incentives are introduced, they are usually preceded by a reorganisation of working methods and it is from this reorganisation that the greatest improvement in labour performance is obtained. Many arguments have been advanced for and against particular types of incentives, but whatever scheme is thought to be the most desirable, it is essential that it does not inhibit the development of effective methods of operation and control. Payment by results should not be considered to be the only incentive, since there is ample evidence that money is only one of many factors influencing worker performance.

Research into motivational factors in British industry has been meagre, but what studies there have been, indicate the importance of job design and delegation of responsibility. Where monetary incentives are considered vital to improved worker performance (five-sixths of British manufacturing industry seem to think so), then it must be re-emphasised that there is no substitute for painstaking and comprehensive studies by competent practitioners. This also applies to the restructuring of wage and salary levels. We advocate that equitable incentive plans should relate to productivity improvement measured in terms of added value because added value is a function of both capital and labour and involves all within the company organisation. The principles for such a plan should be based upon:

(1) security of job and earnings

(2) evaluation, to stabilise earnings and differentials

(3) worth of the company achieved through the generation of added value

(4) performance, where this is directly contributed by employees

It is important to bear in mind that improving productivity is not just a matter of higher wages, incentives and the excellence of labour relations. We are aware that they go some way towards encouraging improvement, but there are still areas within manufacturing companies that need to be cleared of undergrowth that has been generated by history and inconsistent management practices. Before any productivity bargain begins, managements should task themselves to investigate those areas listed at the end of Chapter 11, and we consider that they will provide a great contribution to productivity and the profitability.

There are many concepts of productivity and nearly as many views on what influences it. While there has been extensive work diagnosing and developing managerial, social and economic models, there has been insufficient effort applied to the integration of costing and productivity measurement techniques. Few economists have ever involved themselves in physical measurements to determine the significant factors that influence productivity. The amount of attention given to management accounting systems by people, other than accountants, leaves much to be desired. Few production engineer managers show interest in the development of new and improved costing criteria, especially relating to the functions of decision and control. All too frequently costing systems are taken for granted, though managements regularly complain about their inadequacy. The design and development of a costing system is far too important a field to be left to the accountant alone. To be effective it should involve a partnership with the engineering management functions. Ultimately, productivity indices should become supreme indicators for economic growth, profits and earnings, at departmental, company, industrial, regional and national levels.

An encouraging feature of this research work has been the enthusiasm of companies in the West Midlands, Yorkshire and Humberside regions to put into effect revised systems of management information and production methods by:

(1) applying low cost automation by mechanising manufacturing processes and assembly methods with inexpensive and readily available automatic control devices

(2) applying modern principles of plant layout and work station design, with the aid of group technology and method study techniques

(3) reducing the variety of products manufactured

(4) planning and controlling production and inventory levels more adequately

(5) arranging consultative practices to improve the relationships and communications between employer and employees

What is now urgent is for industrial managements and trade unionists to co-operate closely with educational and research establishments—to make use of the knowledge, expertise and facilities in the field of production management and together apply themselves to achieve the productivity levels shown in this project to be possible. While it is important to continue the development of production engineering and management degree and diploma course work, as well as specialist training, there will continue to be a need for research as a supporting role. Not only are industrialists starved of modern management information, but university and polytechnic lecturers too are inhibited by the meagre source of modern factual information collected from British manufacturing companies. Most authorities today are forced to rely upon American literature and researches. It is obvious that the need for research into manufacturing is vital, not only for the benefit and development of academic knowledge, but more important for the needs of industry.

References

1 *National Economic Development Council*, 'Conditions Favourable to Foster Growth'. H.M.S.O. (1963)
2 HAROLD WILSON, 'Productivity Survey', *The Financial Times*, June 12 1967
3 JONES, G. and BARNES, M., *Britain on Borrowed Time*, Penguin, London (1967)
4 WELLS, F. A., 'The Relationship between Physical and Financial Comparisons of Productivity', O.E.E.C., Paris (1957)
5 ROSTAS, L., 'Alternative Productivity Concepts', *Productivity Measurement Concepts*, Vol. 1. European Productivity Association (E.P.A.), O.E.C.D., Paris (1955)
6 FOULKE, R., *Practical Financial Statement Analysis*, McGraw-Hill (1968)
7 *The Times*, 29th November 1968
8 BLISS, J. H., *Financial and Operating Ratios in Management*, Ronald Press, New York (1924)
9 WITSCHEY, R. E., *Accounting Theory and the Accounting Profession*, Prentice-Hall Inc., New Jersey (1966)
10 SIZER, J., *An Insight into Management Accounting*, Penguin, London (1969)
11 INGHAM, H., and HARRINGTON, L. TAYLOR, 'Interfirm Comparisons for Management, *B.I.M.* (1963)
12 *Government White Paper* 'In Place of Strife', H.M.S.O. (1969)
13 MARTIN, H. W., 'Productivity Costing and Control'. *Productivity Measurement Review*, No. 37, May 1964, O.E.C.D., Paris
14 LOMAX, K. S., 'Productivity Measurement', Vol. III. O.E.C.D., Paris
15 FREEDMAN, R., *Marx on Economics*, Penguin, London (1961)
16 SMITH, E. and BEECHING, R., 'Measurement of the Effectiveness of the Productive Unit'. *British Institute of Management*, Winter Proceedings No. 4 (1948/1949)
17 EASTERFIELD, T. E., 'Aims and Methods in Productivity Measurement at Plant Level.' *Productivity Measurement Review* No. 24, O.E.C.D., Paris (1961)
18 MELMAN, S., *Decision Making and Productivity*, Basil Blackwell, Oxford (1958)
19 *Board of Trade*, 'Report on the Census of Production', H.M.S.O. (1958)
20 *Central Statistics Office*, 'Standard Industrial Classification, S.I.C., H.M.S.O. (1968)
21 'International Standard Industrial Classification'. *United Nations Statistical Papers*, Series M, No. 4 (1961)
22 *Department of Economic Affairs*, 'The West Midlands—A Regional Study', H.M.S.O. (1965)

174

23 EASTERFIELD, T. E., 'Productivity Measurement in Great Britain—A Survey of Recent Work', D.S.I.R. (1959)

24 *Central Statistical Office*, 'National Income and Expenditure', H.M.S.O. (1966)

25 'Productivity Measurement and Cost Analysis', *Productivity Measurement Review*, Vol. 1, No. 1, O.E.E.C., Paris (1955)

26 DICKEY, R., *Accountants Cost Handbook*, Ronald Press, New York (1960)

27 *Ministry of Technology*, 'American Pointers to Profitability', *New Technology* No. 15, March (1968)

28 RISK, J. M. S., 'The Effective Use of Capital', *The Production Engineer*, October 1969

29 'Terminology of Production', December 1950, O.E.C.D., Paris

30 BAHIRI, S., and MARTIN, H. W., 'Effective Management through Productivity Costing', *Industrial Commercial Techniques (In-Com-Tec)*, London (1968)

31 CORLETT, E. N., NORMAN, R. G., and SNAITH, J. W., 'Measurement and Incentives in Building Maintenance', *Surveyor and Municipal Engineer*, October 1967

32 SHIMMIN, S., *Payment by Results*, Staples Press, London (1959)

33 *New Left Review* No. 48 (1967)

34 DUDLEY, N. A., 'Output Patterns in Repetitive Tasks', *The Production Engineer*, April 1958

35 DUDLEY, N. A., *Work Measurement: Some Research Studies*, Macmillan, London (1968)

36 NORMAN, R. G., *Techniques of Work Study*, Data Publications, Richmond, Surrey (1963)

37 TAYLOR, F. W., *Shop Management*, Harper, New York (1912)

38 CURRIE, R. M., *Work Study*, Pitman, London (1960)

39 *British Standards Institute*, 'Glossary of Terms in Work Study', B.S. 3138 (1969)

40 GRAHAM, C. F., *Work Measurement and Cost Control*, Pergamon, London (1965)

41 BARNES, R. M., *Motion and Time Study*, Wiley, New York (1949)

42 MARRIOTT, R., *Incentive Payment Systems*, Staples Press, London (1957)

43 MATHEW, T. U., 'The Accuracy and Use of Time Study', *O.R. Quarterly*, Vol. 6, No. 1 (1955)

44 MURRELL, K. F. H., *Ergonomics*, Chapman and Hall, London (1965)

45 I.C.W.A. and I.Prod.E., 'Measurement of Productivity', *The Production Engineer* (1949)

46 LUPTON, T., 'A Sociologist looks at Work Study', *Work Study and Industrial Engineering*, No. 1 (1967)

47 NADLER, G., *Work System Design: The Ideals Concept*, Irwin Holmewood, Illinois (1967)

48 *Ministry of Labour*, 'Efficient Use of Manpower', H.M.S.O. (1967)

49 E.P.A., 'Productivity Measurement Concepts', O.E.E.C., Paris (1955)

50 MAVERICK, L., 'The Proper Formula to Employ in Calculating Productivity', *Productivity Measurement Review*, No. 1, O.E.C.D., Paris (1955)

51 LEONTIEF, W., *Technology and Economic Development*, Penguin (1965)

52 *Engineering Employers' Federation*, 'Productivity Bargaining and the Engineering Industry', Research Paper No. 1, Appendix B (1967)

53 *Board of Trade Journal*, H.M.S.O., January 1966

54 *Industrial Policy Group*, 'Structure and Efficiency of British Industry', C.B.I., (1970)

55 GALLOWAY, D. F., 'The Technology, Economy and Philosophy of Improving Productivity in the Manufacturing Industries', *The Production Engineer*, London (1968)

56 TURNER, H. A., CLARKE, GARFIELD and ROBERTS, G., *Labour Relations in the Motor Industry*, Allen and Unwin, London (1967)

57 HOLLIER, R. H., and CORLETT, E. N., 'Work Flow in Batch Production'. *Problems of Progress in Industry*, H.M.S.O. (1967)

58 BARNES, R. M., *Work Sampling*, Wiley, New York (1964)
59 TIPPETT, L. H. C., Letter to the Editor, *Journal of Time and Motion Study*, March 1959
60 ROWE, A. J., 'Relative versus Absolute Errors in Delay Measurements', *British Management Review*, Vol. 13, No. 1 (1955)
61 *Ministry of Labour*, 'Introduction of Shift Working', H.M.S.O. (1967)
62 YOUNG, H., *Sunday Times*, Jan/Feb 1970
63 TINKER, G. C., 'What Machine Capacity do you really need?', *Metalworking Production*, 20th October 1965
64 TINKER, G. C., 'The Utilisation of Machine Tools'. Research Report No. 23, M.T.I.R.A., Cheshire (1968)
65 STEPHENSON, P., *Accountants Week*, October 1970
66 SWANN, K., 'Management Attitudes and Techniques in the Small Company', unpublished Thesis, University of Bradford (1971)
67 *The Daily Telegraph*, 17th October 1970
68 FROST-SMITH, E. H., and MARTEN, H. R., 'Machine Shop Production Organisation—A Target for Research', *The Production Engineer*, November 1968
69 WELMAN, P., 'When a Takeover Victor Moves In . . .' *The Daily Telegraph*, 24th October 1970
70 *International Labour Office*, 'Higher Productivity in Manufacturing Industries', I.L.O., Geneva (1954)
71 DAVISON, J. P., FLORENCE, P. S., GRAY, B., and ROSS, N. S., *Productivity and Economic Incentives*, Allen and Unwin, London (1958)
72 POHORILLE, M., *Productivity and the System of Labour Remuneration*, edited by Dunlop and Diatchenko, McGraw-Hill, New York (1964)
73 KAPUSTIN, E. I., *Wages as an Important Condition for the Growth of Labour Productivity in the U.S.S.R. Labour Productivity*, edited by Dunlop and Diatchenko, McGraw-Hill, New York (1964)
74 BROWN, W., *Piecework Abandoned*, Wiley, New York (1962)
75 MCGREGOR, D., *The Human Side of Enterprise*, McGraw-Hill, New York (1960)
76 LIKERT, R., *New Patterns of Management*, McGraw-Hill, New York (1961)
77 REVANS, R. W., *Science and the Manager*, Macdonald, London (1965)
78 REVANS, R. W., *The Theory of Practice in Management*, Macdonald, London (1966)
79 VROOM, V. H., and DECI, E. L., *Management and Motivation*, Penguin, London (1970)
80 HUMBLE, J., *Management by Objectives*, British Institute of Management, London (1969)
81 ROSS, N. S., *Organised Labour and Management in Human Relations and Modern Management*, Edited by Hugh Jones, E.M. North Holland Publishing Company, Amsterdam (1958)
82 BOYD, J. M., 'Is Industrial Democracy Compatible with Efficiency', *The Production Engineer*, January 1968, London
83 GALBRAITH, J. K., *The New Industrial State*, Hamish Hamilton, London (1967)
84 RUIST, E., 'Productivity, Efficiency and Wages', *Productivity Measurement Review*, Vol. 1, O.E.C.D., Paris (1955)
85 BORCH, K., 'Theories and Principles of Productivity Measurement at Different Levels', *Productivity Measurement Review* No. 42, O.E.C.D., Paris (1965)
86 VITELES, M. S., *Motivation and Morale in Industry*, Staples Press, London (1954)
87 NORMAN, R. G., and SNAITH, J. W., 'Effectiveness of Building Maintenance Organisations'. Five Case Studies presented to the Ministry of Public Building and Works, October 1967
88 HERZBERG, F., *The Motivation to Work*, Wiley, New York (1959)
89 DAVIS, L. E., 'Job Design Factors', *Occupational Psychology* Vol. 34, No. 2 (1960)
90 N.B.P.I. 'Payment by Results Systems' (Supplement) Report No. 65, H.M.S.O. (1969)

176

91 NORRIS, A., 'Job Evaluation', *Industrial Administration and Engineering Production Group*. The Institute of Mechanical Engineers (1965)
92 BAILEY, J. I., Conference on the Maintenance of Buildings: Ministry of Public Building and Works (1966)
93 SCANLON, H., *New Left Review* No. 46 (1967). Cited by Topham, The Institute for Worker Control, Pamphlet Series No. 2
94 CORFIELD, T., T. and G.W.U. Journal, *The Record*, January 1968. Cited by Topham, The Institute for Worker Control, Pamphlet Series No. 2
95 NEALE, F. J., 'Survey on Incentive Payments, First Report Findings', *Institute of Works Management* (1966)
96 N.B.P.I., 'Productivity Agreements' Report No. 36, H.M.S.O. (1967)
97 FLANDERS, A., *The Fawley Productivity Agreement: A case study of Management and Collective Bargaining*, Faber, London (1964)
98 DEWDNEY, D. A. C., 'Productivity Agreements—A Challenge to Management'. *Work Study and Management Services Journal of the Institute of Work Study Practitioners* (1969)
99 *Engineering Employers' Federation*, 'Productivity Bargaining and the Engineering Industry'. Federation Research Paper, No. 1, (1968)
100 N.B.P.I. 'Job Evaluation' Report No. 83. H.M.S.O. (1968)
101 OTIS, L. J., and LEUKART, H. R., *Job Evaluations*, Prentice Hall, New York (1948)
102 GOMBERG, W., *Trades Unions and Industrial Engineering*, Handbook of Industrial Engineering, Prentice Hall, New York (1955)
103 MORTIMER, J., 'Pay and Productivity', Work Study and Management Services. *Journal of the Institute of Work Study Practitioners*, May 1969
104 I.L.O., 'Job Evaluation', International Labour Office, Geneva (1960)
105 SMYTHE, R. C., and MURPHY, M. J., *Job Evaluation and Employee Rating*, McGraw-Hill, New York (1946)
106 LYTTLE, C. W., *Job Evaluation Methods*, Ronald Press, New York (1946)
107 TIFFIN, J., and MCCORMICK, E. J., *Industrial Psychology*, Allen and Unwin, London (1965)
108 JAQUES, E., *Equitable Payment*, Penguin, London (1967)
109 DUDLEY, N. A., 'Research Note: Comparative Productivity Analysis', *International Journal of Production Research*, Vol. 8, London (1970)
110 BROADWAY, F., *State Intervention in British Industry* 1964–1968, Kaye and Ward, London (1969)

Index